FOREIGN AFFAIRS
Special Collection

MASTERS OF INTERNATIONAL RELATIONS

Introduction

Gideon Rose

Sometimes big names are just big names—and sometimes reputations are deserved. In this collection, we've decided to gather together a few of our most recent articles from some of the leading lights in international relations, showing just how the gap between scholars and policymakers can and should be bridged.

It's probably fair to say that most practitioners and general readers find little of interest or value in most contemporary academic work in the social sciences, and that most social scientists are either unconcerned by such attitudes or attribute them to the failings of the consumers, not the producers. However, we here at *Foreign Affairs*—responsible for running a forum for policymakers, scholars, and general readers alike—believe strongly that intellectual rigor, practical relevance, and accessible presentation are not mutually exclusive. We believe, in fact, that when done right, they are actually mutually reinforcing.

Any theory worth its salt will have some practical implications for human life and action, particularly theories in political science and international relations, and drawing out those practical implications, making them clear and vivid, should be a no-brainer part of the standard scholarly task. It is the only serious way to answer the most crucial question of all: Why should I care about this work?

Similarly, presenting arguments transparently and accessibly is not just the best way to give them wings but is also useful for testing and improving them. Abstraction, jargon, and obscurity—unfortunately so common these days as the hallmarks of mainstream academic discourse—are the enemies of thought and truth. As George Orwell famously noted, "If you simplify your English,

GIDEON ROSE is Editor of *Foreign Affairs*.

you are freed from the worst follies of orthodoxy. You cannot speak any of the necessary dialects, and when you make a stupid remark its stupidity will be obvious, even to yourself."

So we see a crucial part of our mission as encouraging leading scholars to leverage their academic expertise and bring it to bear on practical policy issues, presenting their articles in plain language that is accessible and appealing to a broad audience. To that end, this collection includes a wide range of work from prominent scholars and thinkers, spanning across everything from the direction of history and the future of American hegemony, to the handling of immediate policy questions such as the Iranian nuclear program, to the source of humanitarianism and the role of religion in the American polity.

The collection kicks off with Francis Fukuyama revisiting his most famous work on historical teleology, offering his thoughts on "The Future of History." Then comes John Ikenberry discussing "The Future of the Liberal World Order," Joseph Nye examining "The Future of American Power," and Robert Keohane analyzing "Hegemony and After." Fareed Zakaria closes this section with his answer to the question, "Can America Be Fixed?"

The future of U.S. grand strategy is a perennial concern, dealt with here by a debate between Stephen Brooks, John Ikenberry, and William Wohlforth ("Lean Forward") on the one hand and Barry Posen ("Pull Back") on the other. Kenneth Waltz, Robert Jervis, and Richard Betts all chime in on Iran policy in "Why Iran Should Get the Bomb," "Getting to Yes With Iran," and "The Lost Logic of Deterrence," respectively, and Graham Allison offers insights on "The Cuban Missile Crisis at 50."

The collection concludes with Michael Walzer ruminating "On Humanitarianism" and David Campbell and Robert Putnam exploring "God and Caesar in America."

We leave to others the question of whether such pieces should be given any sort of consideration in an academic's official standing. All we will say is that we are proud to have them in our pages and will continue to try to generate more like them in the future.

The Future of History

Can Liberal Democracy Survive the Decline of the Middle Class?

Francis Fukuyama

Something strange is going on in the world today. The global financial crisis that began in 2008 and the ongoing crisis of the euro are both products of the model of lightly regulated financial capitalism that emerged over the past three decades. Yet despite widespread anger at Wall Street bailouts, there has been no great upsurge of left-wing American populism in response. It is conceivable that the Occupy Wall Street movement will gain traction, but the most dynamic recent populist movement to date has been the right-wing Tea Party, whose main target is the regulatory state that seeks to protect ordinary people from financial speculators. Something similar is true in Europe as well, where the left is anemic and right-wing populist parties are on the move.

There are several reasons for this lack of left-wing mobilization, but chief among them is a failure in the realm of ideas. For the past generation, the ideological high ground on economic issues has been held by a libertarian right. The left has not been able to make a plausible case for an agenda other than a return to an unaffordable form of old-fashioned social democracy. This absence of a plausible progressive counternarrative is unhealthy, because competition is

FRANCIS FUKUYAMA is a Senior Fellow at the Center on Democracy, Development, and the Rule of Law at Stanford University and the author, most recently, of *The Origins of Political Order: From Prehuman Times to the French Revolution*.

good for intellectual debate just as it is for economic activity. And serious intellectual debate is urgently needed, since the current form of globalized capitalism is eroding the middle-class social base on which liberal democracy rests.

THE DEMOCRATIC WAVE

Social forces and conditions do not simply "determine" ideologies, as Karl Marx once maintained, but ideas do not become powerful unless they speak to the concerns of large numbers of ordinary people. Liberal democracy is the default ideology around much of the world today in part because it responds to and is facilitated by certain socioeconomic structures. Changes in those structures may have ideological consequences, just as ideological changes may have socioeconomic consequences.

Almost all the powerful ideas that shaped human societies up until the past 300 years were religious in nature, with the important exception of Confucianism in China. The first major secular ideology to have a lasting worldwide effect was liberalism, a doctrine associated with the rise of first a commercial and then an industrial middle class in certain parts of Europe in the seventeenth century. (By "middle class," I mean people who are neither at the top nor at the bottom of their societies in terms of income, who have received at least a secondary education, and who own either real property, durable goods, or their own businesses.)

As enunciated by classic thinkers such as Locke, Montesquieu, and Mill, liberalism holds that the legitimacy of state authority derives from the state's ability to protect the individual rights of its citizens and that state power needs to be limited by the adherence to law. One of the fundamental rights to be protected is that of private property; England's Glorious Revolution of 1688–89 was critical to the development of modern liberalism because it first established the constitutional principle that the state could not legitimately tax its citizens without their consent.

At first, liberalism did not necessarily imply democracy. The Whigs who supported the constitutional settlement of 1689 tended to be the wealthiest property owners in England; the parliament of that period represented less than ten percent of the whole population. Many classic liberals, including Mill, were highly skeptical of the virtues of democracy: they believed that responsible political participation required education and a stake in society—that is, property ownership. Up through the end of the nineteenth century, the franchise was limited by property and educational requirements in virtually all parts of Europe. Andrew Jackson's election as U.S. president in 1828 and his subsequent abolition of property requirements for voting, at least for white males, thus marked an important early victory for a more robust democratic principle.

In Europe, the exclusion of the vast majority of the population from political power and the rise of an industrial working class paved the way for Marxism. *The Communist Manifesto* was published in 1848, the same year that revolutions spread to all the major European countries save the United Kingdom. And so began a century of competition for the leadership of the democratic movement between communists, who were willing to jettison procedural democracy (multiparty elections) in favor of what they believed was substantive democracy (economic redistribution), and liberal democrats, who believed in expanding political participation while maintaining a rule of law protecting individual rights, including property rights.

At stake was the allegiance of the new industrial working class. Early Marxists believed they would win by sheer force of numbers: as the franchise was expanded in the late nineteenth century, parties such as the United Kingdom's Labour and Germany's Social Democrats grew by leaps and bounds and threatened the hegemony of both conservatives and traditional liberals. The rise of the working class was fiercely resisted, often by nondemocratic means; the communists and many socialists, in turn, abandoned formal democracy in favor of a direct seizure of power.

Throughout the first half of the twentieth century, there was a strong consensus on the progressive left that some form of socialism—government control of the commanding heights of the economy in order to ensure an egalitarian distribution of wealth—was unavoidable for all advanced countries. Even a conservative economist such as Joseph Schumpeter could write in his 1942 book, *Capitalism, Socialism, and Democracy*, that socialism would emerge victorious because capitalist society was culturally self-undermining. Socialism was believed to represent the will and interests of the vast majority of people in modern societies.

Yet even as the great ideological conflicts of the twentieth century played themselves out on a political and military level, critical changes were happening on a social level that undermined the Marxist scenario. First, the real living standards of the industrial working class kept rising, to the point where many workers or their children were able to join the middle class. Second, the relative size of the working class stopped growing and actually began to decline, particularly in the second half of the twentieth century, when services began to displace manufacturing in what were labeled "postindustrial" economies. Finally, a new group of poor or disadvantaged people emerged below the industrial working class—a heterogeneous mixture of racial and ethnic minorities, recent immigrants, and socially excluded groups, such as women, gays, and the disabled. As a result of these changes, in most industrialized societies, the old working class has become just another domestic interest group, one using the political power of trade unions to protect the hard-won gains of an earlier era.

Economic class, moreover, turned out not to be a great banner under which to mobilize populations in advanced industrial countries for political action. The Second International got a rude wake-up call in 1914, when the working classes of Europe abandoned calls for class warfare and lined up behind conservative leaders preaching nationalist slogans, a pattern that persists to the present day. Many Marxists tried to explain this, according to the scholar Ernest Gellner, by what he dubbed the "wrong address theory":

> Just as extreme Shi'ite Muslims hold that Archangel Gabriel made a mistake, delivering the Message to Mohamed when it was intended for Ali, so Marxists basically like to think that the spirit of history or

> human consciousness made a terrible boob. The awakening message was intended for classes, but by some terrible postal error was delivered to nations.

Gellner went on to argue that religion serves a function similar to nationalism in the contemporary Middle East: it mobilizes people effectively because it has a spiritual and emotional content that class consciousness does not. Just as European nationalism was driven by the shift of Europeans from the countryside to cities in the late nineteenth century, so, too, Islamism is a reaction to the urbanization and displacement taking place in contemporary Middle Eastern societies. Marx's letter will never be delivered to the address marked "class."

Marx believed that the middle class, or at least the capital-owning slice of it that he called the bourgeoisie, would always remain a small and privileged minority in modern societies. What happened instead was that the bourgeoisie and the middle class more generally ended up constituting the vast majority of the populations of most advanced countries, posing problems for socialism. From the days of Aristotle, thinkers have believed that stable democracy rests on a broad middle class and that societies with extremes of wealth and poverty are susceptible either to oligarchic domination or populist revolution. When much of the developed world succeeded in creating middle-class societies, the appeal of Marxism vanished. The only places where leftist radicalism persists as a powerful force are in highly unequal areas of the world, such as parts of Latin America, Nepal, and the impoverished regions of eastern India.

What the political scientist Samuel Huntington labeled the "third wave" of global democratization, which began in southern Europe in the 1970s and culminated in the fall of communism in Eastern Europe in 1989, increased the number of electoral democracies around the world from around 45 in 1970 to more than 120 by the late 1990s. Economic growth has led to the emergence of new middle classes in countries such as Brazil, India, Indonesia, South Africa, and Turkey. As the economist Moisés Naím has pointed out, these middle classes are relatively well educated, own property, and are technologically connected to the outside world. They are demanding of their governments and mobilize easily as a result of their access to technology. It should not be surprising that the chief instigators of the Arab Spring uprisings were well-educated Tunisians and Egyptians whose expectations for jobs and political participation were stymied by the dictatorships under which they lived.

Middle-class people do not necessarily support democracy in principle: like everyone else, they are self-interested actors who want to protect their property and position. In countries such as China and Thailand, many middle-class people feel threatened by the redistributive demands of the poor and hence have lined up in support of authoritarian governments that protect their class interests. Nor is it the case that democracies necessarily meet the expectations of their own middle classes, and when they do not, the middle classes can become restive.

THE LEAST BAD ALTERNATIVE?

There is today a broad global consensus about the legitimacy, at least in principle, of liberal democracy. In the words of the economist Amartya Sen, "While democracy is not yet universally practiced, nor indeed uniformly accepted, in the general climate of world opinion, democratic governance has now achieved the status of being taken to be generally right." It is most broadly accepted in countries that have reached a level of material prosperity sufficient to allow a majority of their citizens to think of themselves as middle class, which is why there tends to be a correlation between high levels of development and stable democracy.

Some societies, such as Iran and Saudi Arabia, reject liberal democracy in favor of a form of Islamic theocracy. Yet these regimes are developmental dead ends, kept alive only because they sit atop vast pools of oil. There was at one time a large Arab exception to the third wave, but the Arab Spring has shown that Arab publics can be mobilized against dictatorship just as readily as those in

Eastern Europe and Latin America were. This does not of course mean that the path to a well-functioning democracy will be easy or straightforward in Tunisia, Egypt, or Libya, but it does suggest that the desire for political freedom and participation is not a cultural peculiarity of Europeans and Americans.

The single most serious challenge to liberal democracy in the world today comes from China, which has combined authoritarian government with a partially marketized economy. China is heir to a long and proud tradition of high-quality bureaucratic government, one that stretches back over two millennia. Its leaders have managed a hugely complex transition from a centralized, Soviet-style planned economy to a dynamic open one and have done so with remarkable competence—more competence, frankly, than U.S. leaders have shown in the management of their own macroeconomic policy recently. Many people currently admire the Chinese system not just for its economic record but also because it can make large, complex decisions quickly, compared with the agonizing policy paralysis that has struck both the United States and Europe in the past few years. Especially since the recent financial crisis, the Chinese themselves have begun touting the "China model" as an alternative to liberal democracy.

This model is unlikely to ever become a serious alternative to liberal democracy in regions outside East Asia, however. In the first place, the model is culturally specific: the Chinese government is built around a long tradition of meritocratic recruitment, civil service examinations, a high emphasis on education, and deference to technocratic authority. Few developing countries can hope to emulate this model; those that have, such as Singapore and South Korea (at least in an earlier period), were already within the Chinese cultural zone. The Chinese themselves are skeptical about whether their model can be exported; the so-called Beijing consensus is a Western invention, not a Chinese one.

It is also unclear whether the model can be sustained. Neither export-driven growth nor the top-down approach to decision-making will continue to yield good results forever. The fact that the Chinese government would not permit open discussion of the disastrous high-speed rail accident last summer and could not bring the Railway Ministry responsible for it to heel suggests that there are other time bombs hidden behind the façade of efficient decision-making.

Finally, China faces a great moral vulnerability down the road. The Chinese government does not force its officials to respect the basic dignity of its citizens. Every week, there are new protests about land seizures, environmental violations, or gross corruption on the part of some official. While the country is growing rapidly, these abuses can be swept under the carpet. But rapid growth will not continue forever, and the government will have to pay a price in pent-up anger. The regime no longer has any guiding ideal around which it is organized; it is run by a Communist Party supposedly committed to equality that presides over a society marked by dramatic and growing inequality.

So the stability of the Chinese system can in no way be taken for granted. The Chinese government argues that its citizens are culturally different and will always prefer benevolent, growth-promoting dictatorship to a messy democracy that threatens social stability. But it is unlikely that a spreading middle class will behave all that differently in China from the way it has behaved in other parts of the world. Other authoritarian regimes may be trying to emulate China's success, but there is little chance that much of the world will look like today's China 50 years down the road.

DEMOCRACY'S FUTURE

There is a broad correlation among economic growth, social change, and the hegemony of liberal democratic ideology in the world today. And at the moment, no plausible rival ideology looms. But some very troubling economic and social trends, if they continue, will both threaten the stability of contemporary liberal democracies and dethrone democratic ideology as it is now understood.

The sociologist Barrington Moore once flatly asserted, "No bourgeois, no democracy." The Marxists didn't get their communist utopia because mature capitalism generated middle-class societies, not working-class ones. But what if the further development of technology and globalization undermines the middle class and makes it impossible for more than a minority of citizens in an advanced society to achieve middle-class status?

There are already abundant signs that such a phase of development has begun. Median incomes in the United States have been stagnating in real terms since the 1970s. The economic impact of this stagnation has been softened to some extent by the fact that most U.S. households have shifted to two income earners in the past generation. Moreover, as the economist Raghuram Rajan has persuasively argued, since Americans are reluctant to engage in straightforward redistribution, the United States has instead attempted a highly dangerous and inefficient form of redistribution over the past generation by subsidizing mortgages for low-income households. This trend, facilitated by a flood of liquidity pouring in from China and other countries, gave many ordinary Americans the illusion that their standards of living were rising steadily during the past decade. In this respect, the bursting of the housing bubble in 2008–9 was nothing more than a cruel reversion to the mean. Americans may today benefit from cheap cell phones, inexpensive clothing, and Facebook, but they increasingly cannot afford their own homes, or health insurance, or comfortable pensions when they retire.

A more troubling phenomenon, identified by the venture capitalist Peter Thiel and the economist Tyler Cowen, is that the benefits of the most recent waves of technological innovation have accrued disproportionately to the most talented and well-educated members of society. This phenomenon helped cause the massive growth of inequality in the United States over the past generation. In 1974, the top one percent of families took home nine percent of GDP; by 2007, that share had increased to 23.5 percent.

Trade and tax policies may have accelerated this trend, but the real villain here is technology. In earlier phases of industrialization—the ages of textiles, coal, steel, and the internal combustion engine—the benefits of technological changes almost always flowed down in significant ways to the rest of society in terms of employment. But this is not a law of nature. We are today living in what the scholar Shoshana Zuboff has labeled "the age of the smart machine," in which technology is increasingly able to substitute for more and higher human functions. Every great advance for Silicon Valley likely means a loss of low-skill jobs elsewhere in the economy, a trend that is unlikely to end anytime soon.

Inequality has always existed, as a result of natural differences in talent and character. But today's technological world vastly magnifies those differences. In a nineteenth-century agrarian society, people with strong math skills did not have that many opportunities to capitalize on their talent. Today, they can become financial wizards or software engineers and take home ever-larger proportions of the national wealth.

The other factor undermining middle-class incomes in developed countries is globalization. With the lowering of transportation and communications costs and the entry into the global work force of hundreds of millions of new workers in developing countries, the kind of work done by the old middle class in the developed world can now be performed much more cheaply elsewhere. Under an economic model that prioritizes the maximization of aggregate income, it is inevitable that jobs will be outsourced.

Smarter ideas and policies could have contained the damage. Germany has succeeded in protecting a significant part of its manufacturing base and industrial labor force even as its companies have remained globally competitive. The United States and the United Kingdom, on the other hand, happily embraced the transition to the postindustrial service economy. Free trade became less a theory than an ideology: when members of the U.S. Congress tried to retaliate with trade sanctions against China for keeping its currency undervalued, they were indignantly charged with protectionism, as if the playing field were already level. There was a lot of happy talk about the wonders of the knowledge economy, and how dirty, dangerous manufacturing jobs would inevitably be replaced by highly educated workers doing creative and interesting things. This was a gauzy veil placed over the hard facts of deindustrialization. It overlooked the fact that the benefits of the new order accrued disproportionately to a very small number of people in finance and high technology, interests that dominated the media and the general political conversation.

THE ABSENT LEFT

One of the most puzzling features of the world in the aftermath of the financial crisis is that so far, populism has taken primarily a right-wing form, not a left-wing one.

In the United States, for example, although the Tea Party is anti-elitist in its rhetoric, its members vote for conservative politicians who serve the interests of precisely those financiers and corporate elites they claim to despise. There are many explanations for this phenomenon. They include a deeply embedded belief in equality of opportunity rather than equality of outcome and the fact that cultural issues, such as abortion and gun rights, crosscut economic ones.

But the deeper reason a broad-based populist left has failed to materialize is an intellectual one. It has been several decades since anyone on the left has been able to articulate, first, a coherent analysis of what happens to the structure of advanced societies as they undergo economic change and, second, a realistic agenda that has any hope of protecting a middle-class society.

The main trends in left-wing thought in the last two generations have been, frankly, disastrous as either conceptual frameworks or tools for mobilization. Marxism died many years ago, and the few old believers still around are ready for nursing homes. The academic left replaced it with postmodernism, multiculturalism, feminism, critical theory, and a host of other fragmented intellectual trends that are more cultural than economic in focus. Postmodernism begins with a denial of the possibility of any master narrative of history or society, undercutting its own authority as a voice for the majority of citizens who feel betrayed by their elites. Multiculturalism validates the victimhood of virtually every out-group. It is impossible to generate a mass progressive movement on the basis of such a motley coalition: most of the working- and lower-middle-class citizens victimized by the system are culturally conservative and would be embarrassed to be seen in the presence of allies like this.

Whatever the theoretical justifications underlying the left's agenda, its biggest problem is a lack of credibility. Over the past two generations, the mainstream left has followed a social democratic program that centers on the state provision of a variety of services, such as pensions, health care, and education. That model is now exhausted: welfare states have become big, bureaucratic, and inflexible; they are often captured by the very organizations that administer them, through public-sector unions; and, most important, they are fiscally unsustainable given the aging of populations virtually everywhere in the developed world. Thus, when existing social democratic parties come to power, they no longer aspire to be more than custodians of a welfare state that was created decades ago; none has a new, exciting agenda around which to rally the masses.

AN IDEOLOGY OF THE FUTURE

Imagine, for a moment, an obscure scribbler today in a garret somewhere trying to outline an ideology of the future that could provide a realistic path toward a world with healthy middle-class societies and robust democracies. What would that ideology look like?

It would have to have at least two components, political and economic. Politically, the new ideology would need to reassert the supremacy of democratic politics over economics and legitimate anew government as an expression of the public interest. But the agenda it put forward to protect middle-class life could not simply rely on the existing mechanisms of the welfare state. The ideology would need to somehow redesign the public sector, freeing it from its dependence on existing stakeholders and using new, technology-empowered approaches to delivering services. It would have to argue forthrightly for more redistribution and present a realistic route to ending interest groups' domination of politics.

Economically, the ideology could not begin with a denunciation of capitalism as such, as if old-fashioned socialism were still a viable alternative. It is more the variety of capitalism that is at stake and the degree to which governments should help societies adjust to change. Globalization need be seen not as an inexorable fact of life but rather as a challenge and an opportunity that must be carefully controlled politically. The new ideology would not see markets as an end in themselves; instead, it would value global trade and investment to the extent that they contributed to a flourishing middle class, not just to greater aggregate national wealth.

It is not possible to get to that point, however, without providing a serious and sustained critique of much of the edifice of modern neoclassical economics, beginning with fundamental assumptions such as the sovereignty of individual preferences and that aggregate income is an accurate measure of national well-being. This critique would have to note that people's incomes do not necessarily represent their true contributions to society. It would have to go further, however, and recognize that even if labor markets were efficient, the natural distribution of talents is not necessarily fair and that individuals are not sovereign entities but beings heavily shaped by their surrounding societies.

Most of these ideas have been around in bits and pieces for some time; the scribbler would have to put them into a coherent package. He or she would also have to avoid the "wrong address" problem. The critique of globalization, that is, would have to be tied to nationalism as a strategy for mobilization in a way that defined national interest in a more sophisticated way than, for example, the "Buy American" campaigns of unions in the United States. The product would be a synthesis of ideas from both the left and the right, detached from the agenda of the marginalized groups that constitute the existing progressive movement. The ideology would be populist; the message would begin with a critique of the elites that allowed the benefit of the many to be sacrificed to that of the few and a critique of the money politics, especially in Washington, that overwhelmingly benefits the wealthy.

The dangers inherent in such a movement are obvious: a pullback by the United States, in particular, from its advocacy of a more open global system could set off protectionist responses elsewhere. In many respects, the Reagan-Thatcher revolution succeeded just as its proponents hoped, bringing about an increasingly competitive, globalized, friction-free world. Along the way, it generated tremendous wealth and created rising middle classes all over the developing world, and the spread of democracy in their wake. It is possible that the developed world is on the cusp of a series of technological breakthroughs that will not only increase productivity but also provide meaningful employment to large numbers of middle-class people.

But that is more a matter of faith than a reflection of the empirical reality of the last 30 years, which points in the opposite direction. Indeed, there are a lot of reasons to think that inequality will continue to worsen. The current concentration of wealth in the United States has already become self-reinforcing: as the economist Simon Johnson has argued, the financial sector has used its lobbying clout to avoid more onerous forms of regulation. Schools for the well-off are better than ever; those for everyone else continue to deteriorate. Elites in all societies use their superior access to the political system to protect their interests, absent a countervailing democratic mobilization to rectify the situation. American elites are no exception to the rule.

That mobilization will not happen, however, as long as the middle classes of the developed world remain enthralled by the narrative of the past generation: that their interests will be best served by ever-freer markets and smaller states. The alternative narrative is out there, waiting to be born.

The Future of the Liberal World Order

Internationalism After America

G. John Ikenberry

There is no longer any question: wealth and power are moving from the North and the West to the East and the South, and the old order dominated by the United States and Europe is giving way to one increasingly shared with non-Western rising states. But if the great wheel of power is turning, what kind of global political order will emerge in the aftermath?

Some anxious observers argue that the world will not just look less American—it will also look less liberal. Not only is the United States' preeminence passing away, they say, but so, too, is the open and rule-based international order that the country has championed since the 1940s. In this view, newly powerful states are beginning to advance their own ideas and agendas for global order, and a weakened United States will find it harder to defend the old system. The hallmarks of liberal internationalism—openness and rule-based relations enshrined in institutions such as the United Nations and norms such as multilateralism—could give way to a more contested and fragmented system of blocs, spheres of influence, mercantilist networks, and regional rivalries.

G. JOHN IKENBERRY is Albert G. Milbank Professor of Politics and International Affairs at Princeton University and the author of *Liberal Leviathan: The Origins, Crisis, and Transformation of the American World Order* (Princeton University Press, 2011), from which this essay is adapted.

The fact that today's rising states are mostly large non-Western developing countries gives force to this narrative. The old liberal international order was designed and built in the West. Brazil, China, India, and other fast-emerging states have a different set of cultural, political, and economic experiences, and they see the world through their anti-imperial and anticolonial pasts. Still grappling with basic problems of development, they do not share the concerns of the advanced capitalist societies. The recent global economic slowdown has also bolstered this narrative of liberal international decline. Beginning in the United States, the crisis has tarnished the American model of liberal capitalism and raised new doubts about the ability of the United States to act as the global economic leader.

For all these reasons, many observers have concluded that world politics is experiencing not just a changing of the guard but also a transition in the ideas and principles that underlie the global order. The journalist Gideon Rachman, for example, says that a cluster of liberal internationalist ideas—such as faith in democratization, confidence in free markets, and the acceptability of U.S. military power—are all being called into question. According to this worldview, the future of international order will be shaped above all by China, which will use its growing power and wealth to push world politics in an illiberal direction. Pointing out that China and other non-Western states have weathered the recent financial crisis better than their Western counterparts, pessimists argue that an authoritarian capitalist alternative to Western neoliberal ideas has already emerged. According to the scholar Stefan Halper, emerging-market states "are learning to combine market economics with traditional autocratic or semiautocratic politics in a process that signals an intellectual rejection of the Western economic model."

But this panicked narrative misses a deeper reality: although the United States' position in the global system is changing, the liberal international order is alive and well. The struggle over international order today is not about fundamental principles. China and other emerging great powers do not want to contest the basic rules and principles of the liberal international order; they wish to gain more authority and leadership within it.Indeed, today's power transition represents not the defeat of the liberal order but its ultimate ascendance. Brazil, China, and India have all become more prosperous and capable by operating inside the existing international order—benefiting from its rules, practices, and institutions, including the World Trade Organization (WTO) and the newly organized G-20. Their economic success and growing influence are tied to the liberal internationalist organization of world politics, and they have deep interests in preserving that system.

In the meantime, alternatives to an open and rule-based order have yet to crystallize. Even though the last decade has brought remarkable upheavals in the global system—the emergence of new powers, bitter disputes among Western allies over the United States' unipolar ambitions, and a global financial crisis and recession—the liberal international order has no competitors. On the contrary, the rise of non-Western powers and the growth of economic and security interdependence are creating new constituencies for it.

To be sure, as wealth and power become less concentrated in the United States' hands, the country will be less able to shape world politics. But the underlying foundations of the liberal international order will survive and thrive. Indeed, now may be the best time for the United States and its democratic partners to update the liberal order for a new era, ensuring that it continues to provide the benefits of security and prosperity that it has provided since the middle of the twentieth century.

THE LIBERAL ASCENDANCY

China and the other emerging powers do not face simply an American-led order or a Western system. They face a broader international order that is the product of centuries of struggle and innovation. It is highly developed, expansive, integrated, institutionalized, and deeply rooted in the societies and economies of both advanced capitalist states and developing states. And over the last half century, this order has been unusually capable of assimilating rising powers and reconciling political and cultural diversity.

Today's international order is the product of two order-building projects that began centuries ago. One is the creation and expansion of the modern state system, a project dating back to the Peace of Westphalia in 1648. In the years since then, the project has promulgated rules and principles associated with state sovereignty and norms of great-power conduct. The other project is the construction of the liberal order, which over the last two centuries was led by the United Kingdom and the United States and which in the twentieth century was aided by the rise of liberal democratic states. The two projects have worked together. The Westphalian project has focused on solving the "realist" problems of creating stable and cooperative interstate relations under conditions of anarchy, and the liberal-order-building project has been possible only when relations between the great powers have been stabilized. The "problems of Hobbes," that is, anarchy and power insecurities, have had to be solved in order to take advantage of the "opportunities of Locke," that is, the construction of open and rule-based relations.

At the heart of the Westphalian project is the notion of state sovereignty and great-power relations. The original principles of the Westphalian system—sovereignty, territorial integrity, and nonintervention—reflected an emerging consensus that states were the rightful political units for the establishment of legitimate rule. Founded in western Europe, the Westphalian system has expanded outward to encompass the entire globe. New norms and principles—such as self-determination and mutual recognition among sovereign states—have evolved within it, further reinforcing the primacy of states and state authority. Under the banners of sovereignty and self-determination, political movements for decolonization and independence were set in motion in the non-Western developing world, coming to fruition in the decades after World War II. Westphalian norms have been violated and ignored, but they have, nonetheless, been the most salient and agreed-on parts of the international order.

A succession of postwar settlements—Vienna in 1815, Versailles in 1919, Yalta and Potsdam in 1945, and the U.S., Soviet, and European negotiations that ended the Cold War and reunified Germany in the early 1990s—allowed the great powers to update the principles and practices of their relations. Through war and settlement, the great powers learned how to operate within a multipolar balance-of-power system. Over time, the order has remained a decentralized system in which major states compete and balance against one another. But it has also evolved. The great powers have developed principles and practices of restraint and accommodation that have served their interests. The Congress of Vienna in 1815, where post-Napoleonic France was returned to the great-power club and a congress system was established to manage conflicts, and the UN Security Council today, which has provided a site for great-power consultations, are emblematic of these efforts to create rules and mechanisms that reinforce restraint and accommodation.

The project of constructing a liberal order built on this evolving system of Westphalian relations. In the nineteenth century, liberal internationalism was manifest in the United Kingdom's championing of free trade and the freedom of the seas, but it was limited and coexisted with imperialism and colonialism. In the twentieth century, the United States advanced the liberal order in several phases. After World War I, President Woodrow Wilson and other liberals pushed for an international order organized around a global collective-security body, the League of Nations, in which states would act together to uphold a system of territorial peace. Open trade, national self-determination, and a belief in progressive global change also undergirded the Wilsonian worldview—a "one world" vision of nation-states that would trade and interact in a multilateral system of laws. But in the interwar period of closed economic systems and imperial blocs, this experiment in liberal order collapsed.

After World War II, President Franklin Roosevelt's administration tried to construct a liberal order again, embracing a vision of an open trading system and a global organization in which the great powers would cooperate to keep the peace—the United Nations. Drawing lessons from Wilson's failure and incorporating ideas from the New Deal, American architects of the postwar order also advanced more ambitious ideas about economic and political cooperation, which were embodied in the Bretton Woods institutions. This vision was originally global in spirit and scope, but it evolved into a more American-led and Western-centered system as a result of the weakness of postwar Europe and rising tensions with the Soviet Union. As the Cold War unfolded, the United States took command of the system, adopting new commitments and functional roles in both security and economics. Its own economic and political system became, in effect, the central component of the larger liberal hegemonic order.

Another development of liberal internationalism was quietly launched after World War II, although it took root more slowly and competed with aspects of the Westphalian system. This was the elaboration of the universal rights of man, enshrined in the UN and its Universal Declaration of Human Rights. A steady stream of conventions and treaties followed that together constitute an extraordinary vision of rights, individuals, sovereignty, and global order. In the decades since the end of the Cold War, notions of "the responsibility to protect" have given the international community legal rights and obligations to intervene in the affairs of sovereign states.

Seen in this light, the modern international order is not really American or Western—even if, for historical reasons, it initially appeared that way. It is something much wider. In the decades after World War II, the United States stepped forward as the hegemonic leader, taking on the privileges and responsibilities of organizing and running the system. It presided over a far-flung international order organized around multilateral institutions, alliances, special relationships, and client states—a hierarchical order with liberal characteristics.

But now, as this hegemonic organization of the liberal international order starts to change, the hierarchical aspects are fading while the liberal aspects persist. So even as China and other rising states try to contest U.S. leadership—and there is indeed a struggle over the rights, privileges, and responsibilities of the leading states within the system—the deeper international order remains intact. Rising powers are finding incentives and opportunities to engage and integrate into this order, doing so to advance their own interests. For these states, the road to modernity runs through—not away from—the existing international order.

JOINING THE CLUB

The liberal international order is not just a collection of liberal democratic states but an international mutual-aid society—a sort of global political club that provides members with tools for economic and political advancement. Participants in the order gain trading opportunities, dispute-resolution mechanisms, frameworks for collective action, regulatory agreements, allied security guarantees, and resources in times of crisis. And just as there are a variety of reasons why rising states will embrace the liberal international order, there are powerful obstacles to opponents who would seek to overturn it.

To begin with, rising states have deep interests in an open and rule-based system. Openness gives them access to other societies—for trade, investment, and knowledge sharing. Without the unrestricted investment from the United States and Europe of the past several decades, for instance, China and the other rising states would be on a much slower developmental path. As these countries grow, they will encounter protectionist and discriminatory reactions from slower-growing countries threatened with the loss of jobs and markets. As a result, the rising states will find the rules and institutions that uphold nondiscrimination and equal access to be critical. The World Trade Organization—the most formal and developed institution of the liberal international order—enshrines these rules and norms, and rising states have been eager to join the WTO and gain the rights and protections it affords. China is already deeply enmeshed in the global trading system, with a remarkable 40 percent of its GNP composed of exports—25 percent of which go to the United States.

China could be drawn further into the liberal order through its desire to have the yuan become an international currency rivaling the U.S. dollar. Aside from conferring prestige, this feat could also stabilize China's exchange rate and grant Chinese leaders autonomy in setting macroeconomic policy. But if China wants to make the yuan a global currency, it will need to loosen its currency controls and strengthen its domestic financial rules and institutions. As Barry Eichengreen and other economic historians have noted, the U.S. dollar assumed its international role after World War II not only because the U.S. economy was large but also because the United States had highly developed financial markets and domestic institutions—economic and political—that were stable, open, and grounded in the rule of law. China will feel pressures to establish these same institutional preconditions if it wants the benefits of a global currency.

Internationalist-oriented elites in Brazil, China, India, and elsewhere are growing in influence within their societies, creating an expanding global constituency for an open and rule-based international order. These elites were not party to the grand bargains that lay behind the founding of the liberal order in the early postwar decades, and they are seeking to renegotiate their countries' positions within the system. But they are nonetheless embracing the rules and institutions of the old order. They want the protections and rights that come from the international order's Westphalian defense of sovereignty. They care about great-power authority. They want the protections and rights relating to trade and investment. And they want to use the rules and institutions of liberal internationalism as platforms to project their influence and acquire legitimacy at home and abroad. The UN Security Council, the G-20, the governing bodies of the Bretton Woods institutions—these are all stages on which rising non-Western states can acquire great-power authority and exercise global leadership.

NO OTHER ORDER

Meanwhile, there is no competing global organizing logic to liberal internationalism. An alternative, illiberal order—a "Beijing model"—would presumably be organized around exclusive blocs, spheres of influence, and mercantilist networks. It would be less open and rule-based, and it would be dominated by an array of state-to-state ties. But on a global scale, such a system would not advance the interests of any of the major states, including China. The Beijing model only works when one or a few states opportunistically exploit an open system of markets. But if everyone does, it is no longer an open system but a fragmented, mercantilist, and protectionist complex—and everyone suffers.

It is possible that China could nonetheless move in this direction. This is a future in which China is not a full-blown illiberal hegemon that reorganizes the global rules and institutions. It is simply a spoiler. It attempts to operate both inside and outside the liberal international order. In this case, China would be successful enough with its authoritarian model of development to resist the pressures to liberalize and democratize. But if the rest of the world does not gravitate toward this model, China will find itself subjected to pressure to play by the rules. This dynamic was on display in February 2011, when Brazilian President Dilma Rousseff joined U.S. Treasury Secretary Timothy Geithner in expressing concern over China's currency policy. China can free-ride on the liberal international order, but it will pay the costs of doing so—and it will still not be able to impose its illiberal vision on the world.

In the background, meanwhile, democracy and the rule of law are still the hallmarks of modernity and the global standard for legitimate governance. Although it is true that the spread of democracy has stalled in recent years and that authoritarian China has performed well in the recent economic crisis, there is little evidence that authoritarian states can become truly advanced societies without moving in a liberal democratic direction. The legitimacy of one-party rule within China rests more on the state's ability to deliver economic growth and full employment than on authoritarian—let alone communist—political principles. Kishore Mahbubani, a Singaporean intellectual who has championed China's rise, admits that "China cannot succeed in its goal of becoming a modern developed society until it can take the leap and allow the Chinese people to choose their own rulers." No one knows how far or fast democratic reforms will unfold in China, but a growing middle class, business elites, and human rights groups will exert pressure for them. The Chinese government certainly appears to worry about the long-term preservation of one-party rule, and in the wake of the ongoing revolts against Arab authoritarian regimes, it has tried harder to prevent student gatherings and control foreign journalists.

Outside China, democracy has become a near-universal ideal. As the economist Amartya Sen has noted, "While democracy is not yet universally practiced, nor indeed universally accepted, in the general climate of world opinion democratic governance has achieved the status of being taken to be generally right." All the leading institutions of the global system enshrine democracy as the proper and just form of governance—and no competing political ideals even lurk on the sidelines.

The recent global economic downturn was the first great postwar economic upheaval that emerged from the United States, raising doubts about an American-led world economy and Washington's particular brand of economics. The doctrines of neoliberalism and market fundamentalism have been discredited, particularly among the emerging economies. But liberal internationalism is not the same as neoliberalism or market fundamentalism. The liberal internationalism that the United States articulated in the 1940s entailed a more holistic set of ideas about markets, openness, and social stability. It was an attempt to construct an open world economy and reconcile it with social welfare and employment stability. Sustained domestic support for openness, postwar leaders knew, would be possible only if countries also established social protections and regulations that safeguarded economic stability.

Indeed, the notions of national security and economic security emerged together in the 1940s, reflecting New Deal and World War II thinking about how liberal democracies would be rendered safe and stable. The Atlantic Charter, announced by Roosevelt and Winston Churchill in 1941, and the Bretton Woods agreements of 1944 were early efforts to articulate a vision of economic openness and social stability. The United States would do well to try to reach back and rearticulate this view. The world is not rejecting openness and markets; it is asking for a more expansive notion of stability and economic security.

REASON FOR REASSURANCE

Rising powers will discover another reason to embrace the existing global rules and institutions: doing so will reassure their neighbors as they grow more powerful. A stronger China will make neighboring states potentially less secure, especially if it acts aggressively and exhibits revisionist ambitions. Since this will trigger a balancing backlash, Beijing has incentives to signal restraint. It will find ways to do so by participating in various regional and global institutions. If China hopes to convince its neighbors that it has embarked on a "peaceful rise," it will need to become more integrated into the international order.

China has already experienced a taste of such a backlash. Last year, its military made a series of provocative moves—including naval exercises—in the South China Sea, actions taken to support the government's claims to sovereign rights over contested islands and waters. Many of the countries disputing China's claims joined with the United States at the Regional Forum of the Association of Southeast Asian Nations (ASEAN) in July to reject Chinese bullying and reaffirm open access to Asia's waters and respect for international law. In September, a Chinese fishing trawler operating near islands administered by Japan in the East China Sea rammed into two Japanese coast guard ships. After Japanese authorities detained the trawler's crew, China responded with what one Japanese journalist described as a "diplomatic 'shock and awe' campaign," suspending ministerial-level contacts, demanding an apology, detaining several Japanese workers in China, and instituting a de facto ban on exports of rare-earth minerals to Japan. These actions—seen as manifestations of a more bellicose and aggressive foreign policy—pushed ASEAN, Japan, and South Korea perceptibly closer to the United States.

As China's economic and military power grow, its neighbors will only become more worried about Chinese aggressiveness, and so Beijing will have reason to allay their fears. Of course, it might be that some elites in China are not interested in practicing restraint. But to the extent that China is interested in doing so, it will find itself needing to signal peaceful intentions—redoubling its participation in existing institutions, such as the ASEAN Regional Forum and the East Asia Summit, or working with the other great powers in the region to build new ones. This is, of course, precisely what the United States did in the decades after World War II. The country operated within layers of regional and global economic, political, and security institutions and constructed new ones—thereby making itself more predictable and approachable and reducing the incentives for other states to undermine it by building countervailing coalitions.

More generally, given the emerging problems of the twenty-first century, there will be growing incentives among all the great powers to embrace an open, rule-based international system. In a world of rising economic and security interdependence, the costs of not following multilateral rules and not forging cooperative ties go up. As the global economic system becomes more interdependent, all states—even large, powerful ones—will find it harder to ensure prosperity on their own.

Growing interdependence in the realm of security is also creating a demand for multilateral rules and institutions. Both the established and the rising great powers are threatened less by mass armies marching across borders than by transnational dangers, such as terrorism, climate change, and pandemic disease. What goes on in one country—radicalism, carbon emissions, or public health failures—can increasingly harm another country.

Intensifying economic and security interdependence are giving the United States and other powerful countries reason to seek new and more extensive forms of multilateral cooperation. Even now, as the United States engages China and other rising states, the agenda includes expanded cooperation in areas such as clean energy, environmental protection, nonproliferation, and global economic governance. The old and rising powers may disagree on how exactly this cooperation should proceed, but they all have reasons to avoid a breakdown in the multilateral order itself. So they will increasingly experiment with new and more extensive forms of liberal internationalism.

TIME FOR RENEWAL

Pronouncements of American decline miss the real transformation under way today. What is occurring is not American decline but a dynamic process in which other states are catching up and growing more connected. In an open and rule-based international order, this is what happens. If the architects of the postwar liberal order were alive to see today's system, they would think that their vision had succeeded beyond their wildest dreams. Markets and democracy have spread. Societies outside the West are trading and growing. The United States has more alliance partners today than it did during the Cold War. Rival hegemonic states with revisionist and illiberal agendas have been pushed off the global stage. It is difficult to read these world-historical developments as a story of American decline and liberal unraveling.

In a way, however, the liberal international order has sown the seeds of its own discontent, since, paradoxically, the challenges facing it now—the rise of non-Western states and new transnational threats—are artifacts of its success. But the solutions to these problems—integrating rising powers and tackling problems cooperatively—will lead the order's old guardians and new stakeholders to an agenda of renewal. The coming divide in world politics will not be between the United States (and the West) and the non-Western rising states. Rather, the struggle will be between those who want to renew and expand today's system of multilateral governance arrangements and those who want to move to a less cooperative order built on spheres of influence. These fault lines do not map onto geography, nor do they split the West and the non-West. There are passionate champions of the UN, the WTO, and a rule-based international order in Asia, and there are isolationist, protectionist, and anti-internationalist factions in the West.

The liberal international order has succeeded over the decades because its rules and institutions have not just enshrined open trade and free markets but also provided tools for governments to manage economic and security interdependence. The agenda for the renewal of the liberal international order should be driven by this same imperative: to reinforce the capacities of national governments to govern and achieve their economic and security goals.

As the hegemonic organization of the liberal international order slowly gives way, more states will have authority and status. But this will still be a world that the United States wants to inhabit. A wider array of states will share the burdens of global economic and political governance, and with its worldwide system of alliances, the United States will remain at the center of the global system. Rising states do not just grow more powerful on the global stage; they grow more powerful within their regions, and this creates its own set of worries and insecurities—which is why states will continue to look to Washington for security and partnership. In this new age of international order, the United States will not be able to rule. But it can still lead.

The Future of American Power

Dominance and Decline in Perspective

Joseph S. Nye, Jr.

The twenty-first century began with a very unequal distribution of power resources. With five percent of the world's population, the United States accounted for about a quarter of the world's economic output, was responsible for nearly half of global military expenditures, and had the most extensive cultural and educational soft-power resources. All this is still true, but the future of U.S. power is hotly debated. Many observers have interpreted the 2008 global financial crisis as the beginning of American decline. The National Intelligence Council, for example, has projected that in 2025, "the U.S. will remain the preeminent power, but that American dominance will be much diminished."

Power is the ability to attain the outcomes one wants, and the resources that produce it vary in different contexts. Spain in the sixteenth century took advantage of its control of colonies and gold bullion, the Netherlands in the seventeenth century profited from trade and finance, France in the eighteenth century benefited from its large population and armies, and the United Kingdom in the nineteenth century derived power from its primacy in the Industrial

JOSEPH S. NYE, JR., is University Distinguished Service Professor at Harvard University. Parts of this essay are drawn from his forthcoming book, *The Future of Power* (PublicAffairs, 2011).

Revolution and its navy. This century is marked by a burgeoning revolution in information technology and globalization, and to understand this revolution, certain pitfalls need to be avoided.

First, one must beware of misleading metaphors of organic decline. Nations are not like humans, with predictable life spans. Rome remained dominant for more than three centuries after the peak of its power, and even then it did not succumb to the rise of another state. For all the fashionable predictions of China, India, or Brazil surpassing the United States in the next decades, the greater threat may come from modern barbarians and nonstate actors. In an information-based world, power diffusion may pose a bigger danger than power transition. Conventional wisdom holds that the state with the largest army prevails, but in the information age, the state (or the nonstate actor) with the best story may sometimes win.

Power today is distributed in a pattern that resembles a complex three-dimensional chess game. On the top chessboard, military power is largely unipolar, and the United States is likely to retain primacy for quite some time. On the middle chessboard, economic power has been multipolar for more than a decade, with the United States, Europe, Japan, and China as the major players and others gaining in importance. The bottom chessboard is the realm of transnational relations. It includes nonstate actors as diverse as bankers who electronically transfer funds, terrorists who traffic weapons, hackers who threaten cybersecurity, and challenges such as pandemics and climate change. On this bottom board, power is widely diffused, and it makes no sense to speak of unipolarity, multipolarity, or hegemony.

In interstate politics, the most important factor will be the continuing return of Asia to the world stage. In 1750, Asia had more than half the world's population and economic output. By 1900, after the Industrial Revolution in Europe and the United States, Asia's share shrank to one-fifth of global economic output. By 2050, Asia will be well on its way back to its historical share. The rise of China and India may create instability, but this is a problem with precedents, and history suggests how policies can affect the outcome.

HEGEMONIC DECLINE?

It is currently fashionable to compare the United States' power to that of the United Kingdom a century ago and to predict a similar hegemonic decline. Some Americans react emotionally to the idea of decline, but it would be counterintuitive and ahistorical to believe that the United States will have a preponderant share of power resources forever. The word "decline" mixes up two different dimensions: absolute decline, in the sense of decay, and relative decline, in which the power resources of other states grow or are used more effectively.

The analogy with British decline is misleading. The United Kingdom had naval supremacy and an empire on which the sun never set, but by World War I, the country ranked only fourth among the great powers in its share of military personnel, fourth in GDP, and third in military spending. With the rise of nationalism, protecting the empire became more of a burden than an asset. For all the talk of an American empire, the United States has more freedom of action than the United Kingdom did. And whereas the United Kingdom faced rising neighbors, Germany and Russia, the United States benefits from being surrounded by two oceans and weaker neighbors.

Despite such differences, Americans are prone to cycles of belief in their own decline. The Founding Fathers worried about comparisons to the Roman republic. Charles Dickens observed a century and a half ago, "If its individual citizens, to a man, are to be believed, [the United States] always is depressed, and always is stagnated, and always is at an alarming crisis, and never was otherwise." In the last half century, belief in American decline rose after the Soviet Union launched Sputnik in 1957, after President Richard Nixon's economic adjustments and the oil shocks in the 1970s, and after the closing of rust-belt industries and the budget deficits in the Reagan era. Ten years later, Americans believed that the

United States was the sole superpower, and now polls show that many believe in decline again.

Pundits lament the inability of Washington to control states such as Afghanistan or Iran, but they allow the golden glow of the past to color their appraisals. The United States' power is not what it used to be, but it also never really was as great as assumed. After World War II, the United States had nuclear weapons and an overwhelming preponderance of economic power but nonetheless was unable to prevent the "loss" of China, to roll back communism in Eastern Europe, to overcome stalemate in the Korean War, to stop the "loss" of North Vietnam, or to dislodge the Castro regime in Cuba. Power measured in resources rarely equals power measured in preferred outcomes, and cycles of belief in decline reveal more about psychology than they do about real shifts in power resources. Unfortunately, mistaken beliefs in decline—at home and abroad—can lead to dangerous mistakes in policy.

CHINA ON THE RISE

For more than a decade, many have viewed China as the most likely contender to balance U.S. power or surpass it. Some draw analogies to the challenge that imperial Germany posed to the United Kingdom at the beginning of the last century. A recent book (by Martin Jacques) is even titled *When China Rules the World: The End of the Western World and the Birth of a New Global Order*. Goldman Sachs has projected that the total size of China's economy will surpass that of the United States in 2027.

Yet China has a long way to go to equal the power resources of the United States, and it still faces many obstacles to its development. Even if overall Chinese GDP passed that of the United States around 2030, the two economies, although roughly equivalent in size, would not be equivalent in composition. China would still have a vast underdeveloped countryside, and it would have begun to face demographic problems from the delayed effects of its one-child policy. Per capita income provides a measure of the sophistication of an economy. Assuming a six percent Chinese GDP growth rate and only two percent American GDP growth rate after 2030, China would probably not equal the United States in per capita income until sometime around the middle of the century. In other words, China's impressive economic growth rate and increasing population will likely lead the Chinese economy to pass the U.S. economy in total size in a few decades, but that is not the same as equality.

Moreover, linear projections can be misleading, and growth rates generally slow as economies reach higher levels of development. China's authoritarian political system has shown an impressive capability to harness the country's power, but whether the government can maintain that capability over the longer term is a mystery both to outsiders and to Chinese leaders. Unlike India, which was born with a democratic constitution, China has not yet found a way to solve the problem of demands for political participation (if not democracy) that tend to accompany rising per capita income. Whether China can develop a formula that manages an expanding urban middle class, regional inequality, rural poverty, and resentment among ethnic minorities remains to be seen.

Some have argued that China aims to challenge the United States' position in East Asia and, eventually, the world. Even if this were an accurate assessment of China's current intentions (and even the Chinese themselves cannot know the views of future generations), it is doubtful that China will have the military capability to make this possible anytime soon. Moreover, Chinese leaders will have to contend with the reactions of other countries and the constraints created by China's need for external markets and resources. Too aggressive a Chinese military posture could produce a countervailing coalition among China's neighbors that would weaken both its hard and its soft power.

The rise of Chinese power in Asia is contested by both India and Japan (as well as other states), and that provides a major power advantage to the United States. The U.S.-Japanese alliance and the improvement in U.S.-Indian relations mean that China cannot easily expel the Americans from Asia. From that position of strength, the United States, Japan, India, Australia, and others can engage China and provide incentives for it to play a responsible role, while hedging against the possibility of aggressive behavior as China's power grows.

DOMESTIC DECAY?

Some argue that the United States suffers from "imperial overstretch," but so far, the facts do not fit that theory. On the contrary, defense and foreign affairs expenditures have declined as a share of GDP over the past several decades. Nonetheless, the United States could decline not because of imperial overstretch but because of domestic underreach. Rome rotted from within, and some observers, noting the sourness of current U.S. politics, project that the United States will lose its ability to influence world events because of domestic battles over culture, the collapse of its political institutions, and economic stagnation. This possibility cannot be ruled out, but the trends are not as clear as the current gloomy mood suggests.

Although the United States has many social problems—and always has—they do not seem to be getting worse in any linear manner. Some of these problems are even improving, such as rates of crime, divorce, and teenage pregnancy. Although there are culture wars over issues such as same-sex marriage and abortion, polls show an overall increase in tolerance. Civil society is robust, and church attendance is high, at 42 percent. The country's past cultural battles, over immigration, slavery, evolution, temperance, McCarthyism, and civil rights, were arguably more serious than any of today's.

A graver concern would be if the country turned inward and seriously curtailed immigration. With its current levels of immigration, the United States is one of the few developed countries that may avoid demographic decline and keep its share of world population, but this could change if xenophobia or reactions to terrorism closed its borders. The percentage of foreign-born residents in the United States reached its twentieth-century peak, 14.7 percent, in 1910. Today, 11.7 percent of U.S. residents are foreign born, but in 2009, 50 percent of Americans favored decreasing immigration, up from 39 percent in 2008. The economic recession has only aggravated the problem.

Although too rapid a rate of immigration can cause social problems, over the long term, immigration strengthens U.S. power. Today, the United States is the world's third most populous country; 50 years from now, it is likely to still be third (after India and China). Not only is this relevant to economic power, but given that nearly all developed countries are aging and face the burden of providing for the older generation, immigration could help reduce the sharpness of the resulting policy problem. In addition, there is a strong correlation between the number of H-1B visas and the number of patents filed in the United States. In 1998, Chinese- and Indian-born engineers were running one-quarter of Silicon Valley's high-tech businesses, and in 2005, immigrants were found to have helped start one of every four American technology start-ups over the previous decade.

Equally important are the benefits of immigration for the United States' soft power. Attracted by the upward mobility of American immigrants, people want to come to the United States. The United States is a magnet, and many people can envisage themselves as Americans. Many successful Americans look like people in other countries. Rather than diluting hard and soft power, immigration enhances both. When Singapore's Lee Kuan Yew concludes that China will not surpass the United States as the leading power of the twenty-first century, he cites the ability of the United States to attract the best and brightest from the rest of the world and meld them into a diverse culture of creativity. China has a larger population to recruit from domestically, but in his view, its Sinocentric culture will make it less creative than the United States, which can draw on the whole world.

On the other hand, a failure in the performance of the U.S. economy would be a showstopper. Keeping in mind that macroeconomic forecasts (like weather forecasts) are notoriously unreliable, it appears that the United States will experience slower growth in the decade after the 2008 financial crisis. The International Monetary Fund expects U.S. economic growth to average about two percent in 2014. This is lower than the average over the past several decades but roughly the same as the average rate over the past ten years.

In the 1980s, many observers believed that the U.S. economy had run out of steam and that Germany and Japan were overtaking the United States. The country seemed to have lost its competitive edge. Today, however, even after the financial crisis and the ensuing recession, the World Economic Forum has ranked the United States fourth (after Switzerland, Sweden, and Singapore) in global economic competitiveness. (China, in comparison, was ranked 27th.) The U.S. economy leads in many new growth sectors, such as information technology, biotechnology, and nanotechnology. And even though optimists tend to cite the United States' dominance in the production and use of information technology, that is not the only source of U.S. productivity. The United States has seen significant agricultural innovation, too, and its openness to globalization, if it continues, will also drive up productivity. Economic experts project that American productivity growth will be between 1.5 and 2.25 percent in the next decade.

In terms of investment in research and development, the United States was the world leader in 2007, with $369 billion, followed by all of Asia ($338 billon) and the European Union ($263 billion). The United States spent 2.7 percent of its GDP on research and development, nearly double what China spent (but slightly less than the three percent spent by Japan and South Korea). In 2007, American inventors registered about 80,000 patents in the United States, or more than the rest of the world combined. A number of reports have expressed concern about problems such as high corporate tax rates, the flight of human capital, and the growing number of overseas patents, but U.S. venture capital firms invest 70 percent of their money in domestic start-ups. A 2009 survey by the Global Entrepreneurship Monitor ranked the United States ahead of other countries in opportunities for entrepreneurship because it has a favorable business culture, the most mature venture capital industry, close relations between universities and industry, and an open immigration policy.

Other concerns about the future of the U.S. economy focus on the current account deficit (whose current level indicates that Americans are becoming more indebted to foreigners) and the rise in government debt. In the words of the historian Niall Ferguson, "This is how empires decline. It begins with a debt explosion." Not only did the recent bank bailout and Keynesian stimulus package add to U.S. debt, but the rising costs of health care and entitlement programs such as Social Security, along with the rising cost of servicing the debt, will claim large shares of future revenue. Other observers are less alarmist. The United States, they claim, is not like Greece.

The Congressional Budget Office calculates that total government debt will reach 100 percent of GDP by 2023, and many economists begin to worry when debt levels in rich countries exceed 90 percent. But as The Economist pointed out last June, "America has two huge advantages over other countries that have allowed it to face its debt with relative equanimity: possessing both the world's reserve currency and its most liquid asset market, in Treasury bonds." And contrary to fears of a collapse of confidence in the dollar, during the financial crisis, the dollar rose and bond yields fell. A sudden crisis of confidence is less the problem than that a gradual increase in the cost of servicing the debt could affect the long-term health of the economy.

It is in this sense that the debt problem is important, and studies suggest that interest rates rise 0.03 percent for every one percent increase in the debt-to-GDP ratio over the long term. Higher interest rates mean lower private-sector investment and slower growth. These effects can be mitigated by good policies or exacerbated by bad ones. Increasing debt need not lead to the United States' decline, but it certainly raises the long-term risk.

A well-educated labor force is another key to economic success in the information age. At first glance, the United States does well in this regard. It spends twice as much on higher education as a percentage of GDP as do France, Germany, Japan, and the United Kingdom. The London-based *Times Higher Education's* 2009 list of the top ten universities includes six in the United States, and a 2010 study by Shanghai Jiao Tong University places 17 U.S. universities—and no Chinese universities—among its top 20. Americans win more Nobel Prizes and publish more scientific papers in peer-reviewed journals—three times as many as the Chinese—than do the citizens of any other country. These accomplishments enhance both the country's economic power and its soft power.

American education at its best—many universities and the top slice of the secondary education system—meets or sets the global standard. But American education at its worst—too many primary and secondary schools, especially in less affluent districts—lags badly behind. This means that the quality of the labor force will not keep up with the rising standards needed in an information-driven economy. There is no convincing evidence that students are performing worse than in the past, but the United States' educational advantage is eroding because other countries are doing better than ever. Improvement in the country's K-12 education system will be necessary if the country is to meet the standards needed in an information-based economy.

POLITICS AND INSTITUTIONS

Despite these problems and uncertainties, it seems probable that with the right policies, the U.S. economy can continue to produce hard power for the country. But what about U.S. institutions? The journalist James Fallows, who spent years in China, came home worried less about the United States' economic performance than the gridlock in its political system. In his view, "America still has the means to address nearly any of its structural weaknesses. . . . That is the American tragedy of the early 21st century: a vital and self-renewing culture that attracts the world's talent and a governing system that increasingly looks like a joke." Although political gridlock in a period of recession looks bad, it is difficult to ascertain whether the situation today is much worse than in the past.

Power conversion—translating power resources into desired outcomes—is a long-standing problem for the United States. The U.S. Constitution is based on the eighteenth-century liberal view that power is best controlled by fragmentation and countervailing checks and balances. In foreign policy, the Constitution has always invited the president and Congress to compete for control. Strong economic and ethnic pressure groups struggle for their self-interested definitions of the national interest, and Congress is designed to pay attention to squeaky wheels.

Another cause for concern is the decline of public confidence in government institutions. In 2010, a poll by the Pew Research Center found that 61 percent of respondents thought the United States was in decline, and only 19 percent trusted the government to do what is right most of the time. In 1964, by contrast, three-quarters of the American public said they trusted the federal government to do the right thing most of the time. The numbers have varied somewhat over time, rising after 9/11 before gradually declining again.

The United States was founded in part on a mistrust of government, and its constitution was designed to resist centralized power. Moreover, when asked not about day-to-day government but about the underlying constitutional framework, Americans are very positive. If asked where the best place to live is, the overwhelming majority of them say the United States. If asked whether they like their democratic system of government, nearly everyone says yes. Few people feel the system is rotten and must be overthrown.

Some aspects of the current mood probably represent discontent with the bickering and deadlock in the political process. Compared with the recent past, party politics has become more polarized, but nasty politics is nothing new—as John Adams, Alexander Hamilton, and Thomas Jefferson could attest. Part of the problem with assessing the current atmosphere is that trust in government became abnormally high among the generation that survived the Depression and won World War II. Over the long view of U.S. history, that generation may be the anomaly. Much of the evidence for a loss of trust in government comes from modern polling data, and responses are sensitive to the way questions are asked. The sharpest decline occurred more than four decades ago, during the Johnson and Nixon administrations.

This does not mean that there are no problems with declining confidence in government. If the public became unwilling to pay taxes or comply with laws, or if bright young people refused to go into public service, the government's capacity would be impaired, and people would become more dissatisfied with the government. Moreover, a climate of distrust can trigger extreme actions by deviant members of the population, such as the 1995 bombing of a federal office building in Oklahoma City. Such results could diminish the United States' hard and soft power.

As yet, however, these fears do not seem to have materialized. The Internal Revenue Service has seen no increase in tax cheating. By many accounts, government officials have become less corrupt than in earlier decades, and the World Bank gives the United States a high score (above the 90th percentile) on "control of corruption." The voluntary return of census forms increased to 67 percent in 2000 and was slightly higher in 2010, reversing a 30-year decline. Voting rates fell from 62 percent to 50 percent over the four decades after 1960, but the decline stopped in 2000 and returned to 58 percent in 2008. In other words, the public's behavior has not changed as dramatically as its responses to poll questions indicates.

How serious are changes in social capital when it comes to the effectiveness of American institutions? The political scientist Robert Putnam notes that community bonds have not weakened steadily over the last century. On the contrary, U.S. history, carefully examined, is a story of ups and downs in civic engagement. Three-quarters of Americans, according to the Pew Partnership for Civic Change, feel connected to their communities and say that the quality of life there is excellent or good. Another of the group's polls found that 111 million Americans had volunteered their time to help solve problems in their communities in the past 12 months and that 60 million volunteer on a regular basis. Forty percent said working together with others in their community was the most important thing they could do.

In recent years, U.S. politics and political institutions have become more polarized than the actual distribution of public opinion would suggest. The situation has been exacerbated by the recent economic downturn. As *The Economist* noted, "America's political system was designed to make legislation at the federal level difficult, not easy. . . . So the basic system works; but that is no excuse for ignoring areas where it could be reformed." Some important reforms—such as changing the gerrymandered safe seats in the House of Representatives or altering Senate rules about filibusters—would not require any constitutional amendment. Whether the U.S. political system can reform itself and cope with the problems described above remains to be seen, but it is not as broken as implied by critics who draw analogies to the domestic decay of Rome or other empires.

DEBATING DECLINE

Any net assessment of American power in the coming decades will remain uncertain, but analysis is not helped by misleading metaphors of decline. Declinists should be chastened by remembering how wildly exaggerated U.S. estimates of Soviet power in the 1970s and of Japanese power in the 1980s were. Equally misguided were those prophets of unipolarity who argued a decade ago that the United States was so powerful that it could do as it wished and others had no choice but to follow. Today, some confidently predict that the twenty-first century will see China replace the United States as the world's leading state, whereas others argue with equal confidence that the twenty-first century will be the American century. But unforeseen events often confound such projections. There is always a range of possible futures, not one.

As for the United States' power relative to China's, much will depend on the uncertainties of future political change in China. Barring any political upheaval, China's size and high rate of economic growth will almost certainly increase its relative strength vis-à-vis the United States. This will bring China closer to the United States in power resources, but it does not necessarily mean that China will surpass the United States as the most powerful country—even if China suffers no major domestic political setbacks. Projections based on GDP growth alone are one-dimensional. They ignore U.S. advantages in military and soft power, as well as China's geopolitical disadvantages in the Asian balance of power.

Among the range of possible futures, the more likely are those in which China gives the United States a run for its money but does not surpass it in overall power in the first half of this century. Looking back at history, the British strategist Lawrence Freedman has noted that the United States has "two features which distinguish it from the dominant great powers of the past: American power is based on alliances rather than colonies and is associated with an ideology that is flexible. . . . Together they provide a core of relationships and values to which America can return even after it has overextended itself." And looking to the future, the scholar Anne-Marie Slaughter has argued that the United States' culture of openness and innovation will keep it central in a world where networks supplement, if not fully replace, hierarchical power.

The United States is well placed to benefit from such networks and alliances, if it follows smart strategies. Given Japanese concerns about the rise of Chinese power, Japan is more likely to seek U.S. support to preserve its independence than ally with China. This enhances the United States' position. Unless Americans act foolishly with regard to Japan, an allied East Asia is not a plausible candidate to displace the United States. It matters that the two entities in the world with per capita incomes and sophisticated economies similar to those of the United States—the European Union and Japan—both are U.S. allies. In traditional realist terms of balances of power resources, that makes a large difference for the net position of U.S. power. And in a more positive-sum view of power—that of holding power with, rather than over, other countries—Europe and Japan provide the largest pools of resources for dealing with common transnational problems. Although their interests are not identical to those of the United States, they share overlapping social and governmental networks with it that provide opportunities for cooperation.

On the question of absolute, rather than relative, American decline, the United States faces serious problems in areas such as debt, secondary education, and political gridlock. But they are only part of the picture. Of the multiple possible futures, stronger cases can be made for the positive ones than the negative ones. But among the negative futures, the most plausible is one in which the United States overreacts to terrorist attacks by turning inward and thus cuts itself off from the strength it obtains from openness. Barring such mistaken strategies, however, there are solutions to the major American problems of today. (Long-term debt, for example, could be solved by putting in place, after the economy recovers, spending cuts and consumption taxes that could pay for entitlements.) Of course, such solutions may forever remain out of reach. But it is important to distinguish hopeless situations for which there are no solutions from those that could in principle be solved. After all, the bipartisan reforms of the Progressive era a century ago rejuvenated a badly troubled country.

A NEW NARRATIVE

It is time for a new narrative about the future of U.S. power. Describing power transition in the twenty-first century as a traditional case of hegemonic decline is inaccurate, and it can lead to dangerous policy implications if it encourages China to engage in adventurous policies or the United States to overreact out of fear. The United States is not in absolute decline, and in relative terms, there is a reasonable probability that it will remain more powerful than any single state in the coming decades.

At the same time, the country will certainly face a rise in the power resources of many others—both states and nonstate actors. Because globalization will spread technological capabilities and information technology will allow more people to communicate, U.S. culture and the U.S. economy will become less globally dominant than they were at the start of this century. Yet it is unlikely that the United States will decay like ancient Rome, or even that it will be surpassed by another state, including China.

The problem of American power in the twenty-first century, then, is not one of decline but what to do in light of the realization that even the largest country cannot achieve the outcomes it wants without the help of others. An increasing number of challenges will require the United States to exercise power with others as much as power over others. This, in turn, will require a deeper understanding of power, how it is changing, and how to construct "smart power" strategies that combine hard- and soft-power resources in an information age. The country's capacity to maintain alliances and create networks will be an important dimension of its hard and soft power.

Power is not good or bad per se. It is like calories in a diet: more is not always better. If a country has too few power resources, it is less likely to obtain its preferred outcomes. But too much power (in terms of resources) has often proved to be a curse when it leads to overconfidence and inappropriate strategies. David slew Goliath because Goliath's superior power resources led him to pursue an inferior strategy, which in turn led to his defeat and death. A smart-power narrative for the twenty-first century is not about maximizing power or preserving hegemony. It is about finding ways to combine resources in successful strategies in the new context of power diffusion and "the rise of the rest."

As the largest power, the United States will remain important in global affairs, but the twentieth-century narrative about an American century and American primacy—as well as narratives of American decline—is misleading when it is used as a guide to the type of strategy that will be necessary in the twenty-first century. The coming decades are not likely to see a post-American world, but the United States will need a smart strategy that combines hard- and soft-power resources—and that emphasizes alliances and networks that are responsive to the new context of a global information age.

Hegemony and After

Knowns and Unknowns in the Debate Over Decline

Robert O. Keohane

Playing a dominant role in world politics does not make for an easy life. Even very powerful states encounter problems they cannot solve and situations they would prefer to avoid. But as Macbeth remarks after seeing the witches, "Present fears are less than horrible imaginings." What really scares American foreign policy commentators is not any immediate frustration or danger but the prospect of longer-term decline.

Recently, the United States has been going through yet another bout of declinism—the fifth wave in the last six decades, by the scholar Josef Joffe's count. This one has been caused by the juxtaposition of China's rising power and American economic, political, and military malaise. Just as in the past, however, the surge of pessimism has produced a countersurge of defensive optimism, with arguments put forward about the continued value and feasibility of U.S. global leadership.

Two examples of such antideclinist forays are Robert Kagan's *The World America Made* and Robert Lieber's *Power and Willpower in the American Future*. Both make some cogent points in their analyses of the past, present, and future of the existing U.S.-sponsored global order. But their authors' refusal to accord due weight to multilateral institutions and material power in their assessments

ROBERT O. KEOHANE is Professor of International Affairs at Princeton University.

of that order, and their overconfidence in making assertions about the future, reduce the books' value as appraisals of contemporary world politics.

IT TAKES AN INSTITUTION

Kagan's gracefully written essay notes that the United States has played an essential role in creating the international system of the last 60 years, one in which large-scale warfare has been relatively rare, the global economy has grown at unprecedented rates, and the number of democracies has quadrupled. Harking back to Frank Capra's *It's a Wonderful Life*, Kagan asks readers to imagine what the world would have been like during this period without American leadership and says the answer is clear: much less attractive. U.S. hegemony helped promote peace, prosperity, and political liberalization, and American power continues to be important in maintaining world order.

The World America Made offers a thoroughly conventional reading of world politics, one focusing on the sources and distribution of power in the international system and the ways in which states interpret their interests. The lack of a common government to enforce rules means that order depends on bargaining, which typically involves threats as well as promises. Threats imply some chance of conflict. And so international systems not dominated by a single great power have only rarely managed to sustain peace for long.

General readers might not realize how conventional this interpretation of world politics is, since Kagan strikes a pose of embattled iconoclasm, ignoring most of the major authors who developed the case—such as E. H. Carr, Hans Morgenthau, and Kenneth Waltz—and claiming to refute other scholars with whom he supposedly disagrees, such as G. John Ikenberry and Joseph Nye.

Unfortunately, Kagan's method of disagreement is unconvincing. When he raises an opposing claim, he almost never provides data or even systematic evidence; instead, he relies on a counterassertion with a few carefully selected examples. More annoying, he typically overstates the argument in question, stripping it of its original nuance, before claiming to refute it.

One of his favorite rhetorical tactics is to assert that his opponents think some trend is "inevitable" or "irreversible"—the dominance of the American-led liberal order, the rise of democracy, the end of major war. Another is to suggest that his targets believe in "multipolar harmony." But two of the most basic propositions of contemporary international relations, certainly accepted by all the writers he dismisses, are that world politics is a realm of inherent uncertainty and that it is characterized by a natural absence of harmony. Since practically everybody knows that nothing in world politics is inevitable and harmony is virtually nonexistent, attributing the opposite beliefs to one's opponents assures one of victory in a mock combat.

It is precisely because international discord is the norm, in fact, that theorists and practitioners spend so much time and effort trying to figure out how to generate and sustain cooperation. Many well-informed commentators view the multilateral institutions that have emerged from all this work as providing important supports for the contemporary world order. They point to the roles of UN peacekeeping operations in fostering security, the World Bank in promoting development, the International Monetary Fund (IMF) in enhancing financial stability, the World Trade Organization in fostering commerce, and NATO and the European Union in helping achieve unprecedented peace and unity across an entire continent.

Kagan scoffs, arguing that other states accept U.S. dominance not because it has been embedded in such frameworks but because they approve of American values and goals and believe they may need American power down the road. He disparages the United Nations; ignores UN peacekeeping, the World Bank, and the IMF; and is dismissive of the European Union. But his rejection of the value of institutions is based largely on one sentence, worth quoting in full as an example of his style of argumentation: "All efforts to hand off the maintenance of order and security to an international body with greater authority than the nations within it, or to rely on nations to abide by international rules, regardless of their power to flout them, have failed." Yet Kagan does not mention the fact that the UN Security Council has always operated with the possibility of vetoes by any of the five permanent members—showing that there was never any effort to endow it with authority above those states—nor does he note the extensive literature that explores how states use the UN and other multilateral institutions to pursue their interests, rather than "hand[ing] off" power to them. This is less serious debate than the tossing of cherry bombs at straw men.

The World America Made thus combines a conventional and often sensible analysis of world politics and modern U.S. foreign policy with tendentious criticism of supposedly competing arguments that few, if any, authors actually make. Kagan does not engage in serious analysis of how much military power the United States needs to maintain its central leadership role, in alliance with other democracies, in a stable world order, or of how what Nye has called "soft power" can contribute, in conjunction with "hard" material power, to U.S. influence.

Lieber's book largely agrees with Kagan's, arguing that "the maintenance of [the United States'] leading [international] role matters greatly. The alternative would . . . be a more disorderly and dangerous world." *Power and Willpower in the American Future* documents the many erroneous statements about American decline by commentators such as the historian Paul Kennedy (who argued in 1987 that the United States suffered from "imperial overstretch") and even Henry Kissinger (who wrote in 1961 that "the United States cannot afford another decline like that which has characterized the past decade and a half"). Lieber provides useful data on the relative economic production of major countries and gives both his predecessors and his intellectual opponents due credit for their contributions.

In the end, however, the flaws in Lieber's arguments are similar to those in Kagan's. He, too, dismisses multilateralism as generally ineffective, emphasizing its failures while paying less attention to its successes, whether in peacekeeping, trade, or nonproliferation. He slights NATO's operations in Kosovo in 1999 and Libya in 2011, for example, arguing that the former exhibited "military and tactical limitations" and pointing out that "stronger and more decisive initial attacks" might have brought quicker success in the latter. Even if valid, surely these critiques are relatively minor compared to the results achieved, with high international legitimacy, in both cases. But Lieber has difficulty admitting that such episodes should be counted as evidence for multilateralism rather than against it.

In a previous book, Lieber offered a robust defense of and rationale for the foreign policy approach of the George W. Bush administration, including making a case for preventive war. One might have hoped that in this successor volume he would have revisited such issues and subjected the practical track record of unbridled unilateralism to the same sort of withering scrutiny he gives to multilateralism, but such self-reflection is not to be found here. (Nor is it present in Kagan's book, for that matter, where it would have been equally welcome.)

KNOWN AND UNKNOWN

Apart from questions of originality and the specifics of the declinist debate, the central problem with books of present-oriented foreign policy commentary such as these lies in their failure to distinguish between what is known and what is unknowable. By conflating the two, they end up misleading readers rather than educating them. It might be useful, therefore, to indicate half a dozen things relevant to the future of the U.S. global role that can now be said with confidence.

First, we know that in the absence of leadership, world politics suffers from collective action problems, as each state tries to shift the burdens of adjustment to change onto others. Without alliances or other institutions helping provide reassurance, uncertainty generates security dilemmas, with states eyeing one another suspiciously. So leadership is indeed essential in order to promote cooperation, which is in turn necessary to solve global problems ranging from war to climate change.

Second, we know that leadership is exercised most effectively by creating multilateral institutions that enable states to share responsibilities and burdens. Such institutions may not always succeed in their objectives or eliminate disagreements among their members, but they make cooperation easier and reduce the leader's burdens—which is why policymakers in Washington and many other capitals have invested so much effort for so many decades in creating and maintaining them.

Third, we know that leadership is costly and states other than the leader have incentives to shirk their responsibilities. This means that the burdens borne by the leader are likely to increase over time and that without efforts to encourage sharing of the load, leadership may not be sustainable.

Fourth, we know that in a democracy such as the United States, most people pay relatively little attention to details of policy in general and foreign policy in particular. Pressures for benefits for voters at home—in the form of welfare benefits and tax cuts—compete with demands for military spending and especially nonmilitary foreign affairs spending. This means that in the absence of immediate threats, the public's willingness to invest in international leadership will tend to decline. (A corollary of this point is that advocates of international involvement have incentives to exaggerate threats in order to secure attention and resources.)

Fifth, we know that autocracies are fundamentally less stable than democracies. Lacking the rule of law and accepted procedures for leadership transitions, the former are subject to repeated internal political crises, even though these might play out beneath a unified and stable façade. China's leadership crisis during the spring of 2012, marked by the detention of the politician Bo Xilai and his wife, illustrated this point.

And sixth, we know that among democracies in the world today, only the United States has the material capacity and political unity to exercise consistent global leadership. It has shown a repeated ability to rebound from economic and political difficulties. The size, youth, and diversity of its population; the stability and openness of its political institutions; and the incentives that its economic system creates for innovation mean that it remains the most creative society in the world. Yet it also has major problems—along with intense domestic partisan conflict that prevents those problems from being resolved and that constitutes a major threat to its continued leadership abroad.

What we don't know, however, is at least as important. Will the major powers in the international system, most importantly China, maintain their social and political coherence and avoid civil war? Will the instabilities in the global economy exposed by the 2008 financial crisis be corrected or merely papered over and thus left to cause potential havoc down the road? Will ideologically driven regimes, such as the one in Iran, be prudent or reckless in their quest to develop or even use nuclear weapons, and will potentially threatened states, such as Israel, act prudently in response? Will the trend in recent decades toward greater global democratization be maintained, or will it give way to an antidemocratic reaction? And perhaps most important for the issues discussed here, can the United States as a society summon the political coherence and willpower to devise and implement a sustainable leadership strategy for the twenty-first century?

When it comes to netting out all these factors, declinists are pessimists and antideclinists are optimists. Both camps, however, tend to blend knowledge and speculation and to ground their conclusions more in mood and temperament than in systematic evidence or compelling logic, making it difficult to take their confident claims seriously. Scientists are careful to note the degree of uncertainty associated with their inferences; pundits should seek to follow their example. Given the mix of the known and the unknown, the safest conclusion for readers interested in the next era of world politics is probably the physicist Niels Bohr's injunction not to make predictions, especially about the future.

Can America Be Fixed?

The New Crisis of Democracy

Fareed Zakaria

In November, the American electorate, deeply unhappy with Washington and its political gridlock, voted to maintain precisely the same distribution of power—returning President Barack Obama for a second term and restoring a Democratic Senate and a Republican House of Representatives. With at least the electoral uncertainty out of the way, attention quickly turned to how the country's lawmakers would address the immediate crisis known as the fiscal cliff—the impending end-of-year tax increases and government spending cuts mandated by earlier legislation.

As the United States continues its slow but steady recovery from the depths of the financial crisis, nobody actually wants a massive austerity package to shock the economy back into recession, and so the odds have always been high that the game of budgetary chicken will stop short of disaster. Looming past the cliff, however, is a deep chasm that poses a much greater challenge—the retooling of the country's economy, society, and government necessary for the United States to perform effectively in the twenty-first century. The focus in Washington now is on taxing and cutting; it

FAREED ZAKARIA is the host of Fareed Zakaria GPS on CNN, Editor-at-Large of *Time*, and the author of *The Post-American World*. Follow him on Twitter @FareedZakaria.

should be on reforming and investing. The United States needs serious change in its fiscal, entitlement, infrastructure, immigration, and education policies, among others. And yet a polarized and often paralyzed Washington has pushed dealing with these problems off into the future, which will only make them more difficult and expensive to solve.

Studies show that the political divisions in Washington are at their worst since the years following the Civil War. Twice in the last three years, the world's leading power—with the largest economy, the global reserve currency, and a dominant leadership role in all international institutions—has come close to committing economic suicide. The American economy remains extremely dynamic. But one has to wonder whether the U.S. political system is capable of making the changes that will ensure continued success in a world of greater global competition and technological change. Is the current predicament, in other words, really a crisis of democracy?

That phrase might sound familiar. By the mid-1970s, growth was stagnating and inflation skyrocketing across the West. Vietnam and Watergate had undermined faith in political institutions and leaders, and newly empowered social activists were challenging establishments across the board. In a 1975 report from the Trilateral Commission entitled *The Crisis of Democracy*, distinguished scholars from the United States, Europe, and Japan argued that the democratic governments of the industrial world had simply lost their ability to function, overwhelmed by the problems they confronted. The section on the United States, written by the political scientist Samuel Huntington, was particularly gloomy.

We know how that worked out: within several years, inflation was tamed, the American economy boomed, and confidence was restored. A decade later, it was communism and the Soviet Union that collapsed, not capitalism and the West. So much for the pessimists.

And yet just over two decades further on, the advanced industrial democracies are once again filled with gloom. In Europe, economic growth has stalled, the common currency is in danger, and there is talk that the union itself might split up. Japan has had seven prime ministers in ten years, as the political system splinters, the economy stagnates, and the country slips further into decline. But the United States, given its global role, presents perhaps the most worrying case.

Is there a new crisis of democracy? Certainly, the American public seems to think so. Anger with politicians and institutions of government is much greater than it was in 1975. According to American National Election Studies polls, in 1964, 76 percent of Americans agreed with the statement "You can trust the government in Washington to do what is right just about always or most of the time." By the late 1970s, that number had dropped to the high 40s. In 2008, it was 30 percent. In January 2010, it had fallen to 19 percent.

Commentators are prone to seeing the challenges of the moment in unnecessarily apocalyptic terms. It is possible that these problems, too, will pass, that the West will muddle through somehow until it faces yet another set of challenges a generation down the road, which will again be described in an overly dramatic fashion. But it is also possible that the public is onto something. The crisis of democracy, from this perspective, never really went away; it was just papered over with temporary solutions and obscured by a series of lucky breaks. Today, the problems have mounted, and yet American democracy is more dysfunctional and commands less authority than ever—and it has fewer levers to pull in a globalized economy. This time, the pessimists might be right.

TRENDING NOW

The mid-1970s predictions of doom for Western democracy were undone by three broad economic trends: the decline of inflation, the information revolution, and globalization. In the 1970s, the world was racked by inflation, with rates stretching from low double digits in countries such as the United States and the United Kingdom to 200 percent in countries such as Brazil and Turkey. In 1979, Paul Volcker became chair of the U.S. Federal Reserve, and within a few years, his policies had broken the back of American inflation. Central banks across the world began following the Fed's example, and soon, inflation was declining everywhere.

Technological advancement has been around for centuries, but beginning in the 1980s, the widespread use of computers and then the Internet began to transform every aspect of the economy. The information revolution led to increased productivity and growth in the United States and around the world, and the revolution looks to be a permanent one.

Late in that decade, partly because the information revolution put closed economies and societies at an even greater disadvantage, the Soviet empire collapsed, and soon the Soviet Union itself followed. This allowed the Western system of interconnected free markets and societies to spread across most of the world—a process that became known as globalization. Countries with command or heavily planned economies and societies opened up and began participating in a single global market, adding vigor to both themselves and the system at large. In 1979, 75 countries were growing by at least four percent a year; in 2007, just before the financial crisis hit, the number had risen to 127.

These trends not only destroyed the East but also benefited the West. Low inflation and the information revolution enabled Western economies to grow more quickly, and globalization opened up vast new markets filled with cheap labor for Western companies to draw on and sell to. The result was a rebirth of American confidence and an expansion of the global economy with an unchallenged United States at the center. A generation on, however, the Soviet collapse is a distant memory, low inflation has become the norm, and further advances in globalization and information technology are now producing as many challenges for the West as opportunities.

The jobs and wages of American workers, for example, have come under increasing pressure. A 2011 study by the McKinsey Global Institute found that from the late 1940s until 1990, every recession and recovery in the United States followed a simple pattern. First, GDP recovered to its pre-recession level, and then, six months later (on average), the employment rate followed. But then, that pattern was broken. After the recession of the early 1990s, the employment rate returned to its pre-recession level 15 months after GDP did. In the early part of the next decade, it took 39 months. And in the current recovery, it appears that the employment rate will return to its pre-recession level a full 60 months—five years—after GDP did. The same trends that helped spur growth in the past are now driving a new normal, with jobless growth and declining wages.

MAGIC MONEY

The broad-based growth of the post-World War II era slowed during the mid-1970s and has never fully returned. The Federal Reserve Bank of Cleveland recently noted that in the United States, real GDP growth peaked in the early 1960s at more than four percent, dropped to below three percent in the late 1970s, and recovered somewhat in the 1980s only to drop further in recent years down to its current two percent. Median incomes, meanwhile, have barely risen over the last 40 years. Rather than tackle the underlying problems or accept lower standards of living, the United States responded by taking on debt. From the 1980s on, Americans have consumed more than they have produced, and they have made up the difference by borrowing.

President Ronald Reagan came to power in 1981 as a monetarist and acolyte of Milton Friedman, arguing for small government and balanced budgets. But he governed as a Keynesian, pushing through large tax cuts and a huge run-up in defense spending. (Tax cuts are just as Keynesian as government spending; both pump money into the economy and increase aggregate demand.) Reagan ended his years in office with inflation-adjusted federal spending 20 percent higher than when he started and with a skyrocketing federal deficit. For the 20 years before Reagan, the deficit was under two percent of GDP. In Reagan's two terms, it averaged over four percent of GDP. Apart from a brief period in the late 1990s, when the Clinton administration actually ran a surplus, the federal deficit has stayed above the three percent mark ever since; it is currently seven percent.

John Maynard Keynes' advice was for governments to spend during busts but save during booms. In recent decades, elected governments have found it hard to save at any time. They have run deficits during busts and during booms, as well. The U.S. Federal Reserve has kept rates low in bad times but also in good ones. It's easy to blame politicians for such one-handed Keynesianism, but the public is as much at fault. In poll after poll, Americans have voiced their preferences: they want low taxes and lots of government services. Magic is required to satisfy both demands simultaneously, and it turned out magic was available, in the form of cheap credit. The federal government borrowed heavily, and so did all other governments—state, local, and municipal—and the American people themselves. Household debt rose from $665 billion in 1974 to $13 trillion today. Over that period, consumption, fueled by cheap credit, went up and stayed up.

Other rich democracies have followed the same course. In 1980, the United States' gross government debt was 42 percent of its total GDP; it is now 107 percent. During the same period, the comparable figure for the United Kingdom moved from 46 percent to 88 percent. Most European governments (including notoriously frugal Germany) now have debt-to-GDP levels that hover around 80 percent, and some, such as Greece and Italy, have ones that are much higher. In 1980, Japan's gross government debt was 50 percent of GDP; today, it is 236 percent.

The world has turned upside down. It used to be thought that developing countries would have high debt loads, because they would borrow heavily to finance their rapid growth from low income levels. Rich countries, growing more slowly from high income levels, would have low debt loads and much greater stability. But look at the G-20 today, a group that includes the largest countries from both the developed and the developing worlds. The average debt-to-GDP ratio for the developing countries is 35 percent; for the rich countries, it is over three times as high.

REFORM AND INVEST

When Western governments and international organizations such as the International Monetary Fund offer advice to developing countries on how to spur growth, they almost always advocate structural reforms that will open up sectors of their economies to competition, allow labor to move freely between jobs, eliminate wasteful and economically distorting government subsidies, and focus government spending on pro-growth investment. When facing their own problems, however, those same Western countries have been loath to follow their own advice.

Current discussions about how to restore growth in Europe tend to focus on austerity, with economists debating the pros and cons of cutting deficits. Austerity is clearly not working, but it is just as clear that with debt burdens already at close to 90 percent of GDP, European countries cannot simply spend their way out of their current crisis. What they really need are major structural reforms designed to make themselves more competitive, coupled with some investments for future growth.

Not least because it boasts the world's reserve currency, the United States has more room to maneuver than Europe. But it, too, needs to change. It has a gargantuan tax code that, when all its rules and regulations are included, totals 73,000 pages; a burdensome litigation system; and a crazy patchwork of federal, state, and local regulations. U.S. financial institutions, for example, are often overseen by five or six different federal agencies and 50 sets of state agencies, all with overlapping authority.

If the case for reform is important, the case for investment is more urgent. In its annual study of competitiveness, the World Economic Forum consistently gives the United States poor marks for its tax and regulatory policies, ranking it 76th in 2012, for example, on the "burden of government regulations." But for all its complications, the American economy remains one of the world's most competitive, ranking seventh overall—only a modest slippage from five years ago. In contrast, the United States has dropped dramatically in its investments in human and physical capital. The

WEF ranked American infrastructure fifth in the world a decade ago but now ranks it 25th and falling. The country used to lead the world in percentage of college graduates; it is now ranked 14th. U.S. federal funding for research and development as a percentage of GDP has fallen to half the level it was in 1960—while it is rising in countries such as China, Singapore, and South Korea. The public university system in the United States—once the crown jewel of American public education—is being gutted by budget cuts.

The modern history of the United States suggests a correlation between investment and growth. In the 1950s and 1960s, the federal government spent over five percent of GDP annually on investment, and the economy boomed. Over the last 30 years, the government has been cutting back; federal spending on investment is now around three percent of GDP annually, and growth has been tepid. As the Nobel Prize-winning economist Michael Spence has noted, the United States escaped from the Great Depression not only by spending massively on World War II but also by slashing consumption and ramping up investment. Americans reduced their spending, increased their savings, and purchased war bonds. That boost in public and private investment led to a generation of postwar growth. Another generation of growth will require comparable investments.

The problems of reform and investment come together in the case of infrastructure. In 2009, the American Society of Civil Engineers gave the country's infrastructure a grade of D and calculated that repairing and renovating it would cost $2 trillion. The specific number might be an exaggeration (engineers have a vested interest in the subject), but every study shows what any traveler can plainly see: the United States is falling badly behind. This is partly a matter of crumbling bridges and highways, but it goes well beyond that. The U.S. air traffic control system is outdated and in need of a $25 billion upgrade. The U.S. energy grid is antique, and it malfunctions often enough that many households are acquiring that classic symbol of status in the developing world: a private electrical generator. The country's drinking water is carried through a network of old and leaky pipes, and its cellular and broadband systems are slow compared with those of many other advanced countries. All this translates into slower growth. And if it takes longer to fix, it will cost more, as deferred maintenance usually does.

Spending on infrastructure is hardly a panacea, however, because without careful planning and oversight, it can be inefficient and ineffective. Congress allocates money to infrastructure projects based on politics, not need or bang for the buck. The elegant solution to the problem would be to have a national infrastructure bank that is funded by a combination of government money and private capital. Such a bank would minimize waste and redundancy by having projects chosen by technocrats on merit rather than by politicians for pork. Naturally, this very idea is languishing in Congress, despite some support from prominent figures on both sides of the aisle.

The same is the case with financial reforms: the problem is not a lack of good ideas or technical feasibility but politics. The politicians who sit on the committees overseeing the current alphabet soup of ineffective agencies are happy primarily because they can raise money for their campaigns from the financial industry. The current system works better as a mechanism for campaign fundraising than it does as an instrument for financial oversight.

In 1979, the social scientist Ezra Vogel published a book titled *Japan as Number One*, predicting a rosy future for the then-rising Asian power. When *The Washington Post* asked him recently why his prediction had been so far off the mark, he pointed out that the Japanese economy was highly sophisticated and advanced, but, he confessed, he had never anticipated that its political system would seize up the way it did and allow the country to spiral downward.

Vogel was right to note that the problem was politics rather than economics. All the advanced industrial economies have weaknesses, but they also all have considerable strengths, particularly the United States. They have reached a stage of development, however, at which outmoded policies, structures, and practices have to be changed or abandoned. The problem, as the economist Mancur

Olson pointed out, is that the existing policies benefit interest groups that zealously protect the status quo. Reform requires governments to assert the national interest over such parochial interests, something that is increasingly difficult to do in a democracy.

POLITICAL DEMOGRAPHY

With only a few exceptions, the advanced industrial democracies have spent the last few decades managing or ignoring their problems rather than tackling them head-on. Soon, this option won't be available, because the crisis of democracy will be combined with a crisis of demography.

The industrial world is aging at a pace never before seen in human history. Japan is at the leading edge of this trend, predicted to go from a population of 127 million today to just 47 million by the end of the century. Europe is not far behind, with Italy and Germany approaching trajectories like Japan's. The United States is actually the outlier on this front, the only advanced industrial country not in demographic decline. In fact, because of immigration and somewhat higher fertility rates, its population is predicted to grow to 423 million by 2050, whereas, say, Germany's is predicted to shrink to 72 million. Favorable U.S. demographics, however, are offset by more expensive U.S. entitlement programs for retirees, particularly in the area of health care.

To understand this, start with a ratio of working-age citizens to those over 65. That helps determine how much revenue the government can get from workers to distribute to retirees. In the United States today, the ratio is 4.6 working people for every retiree. In 25 years, it will drop to 2.7. That shift will make a huge difference to an already worrisome situation. Current annual expenditures for the two main entitlement programs for older Americans, Social Security and Medicare, top $1 trillion. The growth of these expenditures has far outstripped inflation in the past and will likely do so for decades to come, even with the implementation of the Affordable Care Act. Throw in all other entitlement programs, the demographer Nicholas Eberstadt has calculated, and the total is $2.2 trillion—up from $24 billion a half century ago, nearly a hundredfold increase.

However worthwhile such programs may be, they are unaffordable on their current trajectories, consuming the majority of all federal spending. The economists Carmen Reinhart and Kenneth Rogoff argued in their detailed study of financial crises, *This Time Is Different*, that countries with debt-to-GDP burdens of 90 percent or more almost invariably have trouble sustaining growth and stability. Unless its current entitlement obligations are somehow reformed, with health-care costs lowered in particular, it is difficult to see how the United States can end up with a ratio much lower than that. What this means is that while the American right has to recognize that tax revenues will have to rise significantly in coming decades, the American left has to recognize that without significant reforms, entitlements may be the only thing even those increased tax revenues will cover. A recent report by Third Way, a Washington-based think tank lobbying for entitlement reform, calculates that by 2029, Social Security, Medicare, Medicaid, and interest on the debt combined will amount to 18 percent of GDP. It just so happens that 18 percent of GDP is precisely what the government has averaged in tax collections over the last 40 years.

The continued growth in entitlements is set to crowd out all other government spending, including on defense and the investments needed to help spur the next wave of economic growth. In 1960, entitlement programs amounted to well under one-third of the federal budget, with all the other functions of government taking up the remaining two-thirds. By 2010, things had flipped, with entitlement programs accounting for two-thirds of the budget and everything else crammed into one-third. On its current path, the U.S. federal government is turning into, in the journalist Ezra Klein's memorable image, an insurance company with an army. And even the army will have to shrink soon.

Rebalancing the budget to gain space for investment in the country's future is today's great American challenge. And despite what one may have gathered during the recent campaign, it is a challenge for both parties. Eberstadt points out that entitlement spending has actually grown faster under Republican presidents than under Democrats, and a *New York Times* investigation in 2012 found that two-thirds of the 100 U.S. counties most dependent on entitlement programs were heavily Republican.

Reform and investment would be difficult in the best of times, but the continuation of current global trends will make these tasks ever tougher and more urgent. Technology and globalization have made it possible to do simple manufacturing anywhere, and Americans will not be able to compete for jobs against workers in China and India who are being paid a tenth of the wages that they are. That means that the United States has no choice but to move up the value chain, relying on a highly skilled work force, superb infrastructure, massive job-training programs, and cutting-edge science and technology—all of which will not materialize without substantial investment.

The U.S. government currently spends $4 on citizens over 65 for every $1 it spends on those under 18. At some level, that is a brutal reflection of democratic power politics: seniors vote; minors do not. But it is also a statement that the country values the present more than the future.

TURNING JAPANESE

Huntington, the author of the section on the United States in the Trilateral Commission's 1975 report, used to say that it was important for a country to worry about decline, because only then would it make the changes necessary to belie the gloomy predictions. If not for fear of Sputnik, the United States would never have galvanized its scientific establishment, funded NASA, and raced to the moon. Perhaps that sort of response to today's challenges is just around the corner—perhaps Washington will be able to summon the will to pass major, far-reaching policy initiatives over the next few years, putting the United States back on a clear path to a vibrant, solvent future. But hope is not a plan, and it has to be said that at this point, such an outcome seems unlikely.

The absence of such moves will hardly spell the country's doom. Liberal democratic capitalism is clearly the only system that has the flexibility and legitimacy to endure in the modern world. If any regimes collapse in the decades ahead, they will be command systems, such as the one in China (although this is unlikely). But it is hard to see how the derailing of China's rise, were it to happen, would solve any of the problems the United States faces—and in fact, it might make them worse, if it meant that the global economy would grow at a slower pace than anticipated.

The danger for Western democracies is not death but sclerosis. The daunting challenges they face—budgetary pressures, political paralysis, demographic stress—point to slow growth rather than collapse. Muddling through the crisis will mean that these countries stay rich but slowly and steadily drift to the margins of the world. Quarrels over how to divide a smaller pie may spark some political conflict and turmoil but will produce mostly resignation to a less energetic, interesting, and productive future.

There once was an advanced industrial democracy that could not reform. It went from dominating the world economy to growing for two decades at the anemic average rate of just 0.8 percent. Many members of its aging, well-educated population continued to live pleasant lives, but they left an increasingly barren legacy for future generations. Its debt burden is now staggering, and its per capita income has dropped to 24th in the world and is falling. If the Americans and the Europeans fail to get their acts together, their future will be easy to see. All they have to do is look at Japan.

Lean Forward

In Defense of American Engagement

Stephen G. Brooks, G. John Ikenberry, and William C. Wohlforth

Since the end of World War II, the United States has pursued a single grand strategy: deep engagement. In an effort to protect its security and prosperity, the country has promoted a liberal economic order and established close defense ties with partners in Europe, East Asia, and the Middle East. Its military bases cover the map, its ships patrol transit routes across the globe, and tens of thousands of its troops stand guard in allied countries such as Germany, Japan, and South Korea.

The details of U.S. foreign policy have differed from administration to administration, including the emphasis placed on democracy promotion and humanitarian goals, but for over 60 years, every president has agreed on the fundamental decision to remain deeply engaged in the world, even as the rationale for that strategy has shifted. During the Cold War, the United States' security

STEPHEN G. BROOKS is Associate Professor of Government at Dartmouth College.

G. JOHN IKENBERRY is Albert G. Milbank Professor of Politics and International Affairs at Princeton University and Global Eminence Scholar at Kyung Hee University in Seoul.

WILLIAM C. WOHLFORTH is Daniel Webster Professor of Government at Dartmouth College. This article is adapted from their essay "Don't Come Home, America: The Case Against Retrenchment," *International Security*, Winter 2012–13.

commitments to Europe, East Asia, and the Middle East served primarily to prevent Soviet encroachment into the world's wealthiest and most resource-rich regions. Since the fall of the Soviet Union, the aim has become to make these same regions more secure, and thus less threatening to the United States, and to use these security partnerships to foster the cooperation necessary for a stable and open international order.

Now, more than ever, Washington might be tempted to abandon this grand strategy and pull back from the world. The rise of China is chipping away at the United States' preponderance of power, a budget crisis has put defense spending on the chopping block, and two long wars have left the U.S. military and public exhausted. Indeed, even as most politicians continue to assert their commitment to global leadership, a very different view has taken hold among scholars of international relations over the past decade: that the United States should minimize its overseas military presence, shed its security ties, and give up its efforts to lead the liberal international order.

Proponents of retrenchment argue that a globally engaged grand strategy wastes money by subsidizing the defense of well-off allies and generates resentment among foreign populations and governments. A more modest posture, they contend, would put an end to allies' free-riding and defuse anti-American sentiment. Even if allies did not take over every mission the United States now performs, most of these roles have nothing to do with U.S. security and only risk entrapping the United States in unnecessary wars. In short, those in this camp maintain that pulling back would not only save blood and treasure but also make the United States more secure.

They are wrong. In making their case, advocates of retrenchment overstate the costs of the current grand strategy and understate its benefits. In fact, the budgetary savings of lowering the United States' international profile are debatable, and there is little evidence to suggest that an internationally engaged America provokes other countries to balance against it, becomes overextended, or gets dragged into unnecessary wars.

The benefits of deep engagement, on the other hand, are legion. U.S. security commitments reduce competition in key regions and act as a check against potential rivals. They help maintain an open world economy and give Washington leverage in economic negotiations. And they make it easier for the United States to secure cooperation for combating a wide range of global threats. Were the United States to cede its global leadership role, it would forgo these proven upsides while exposing itself to the unprecedented downsides of a world in which the country was less secure, prosperous, and influential.

AN AFFORDABLE STRATEGY

Many advocates of retrenchment consider the United States' assertive global posture simply too expensive. The international relations scholar Christopher Layne, for example, has warned of the country's "ballooning budget deficits" and argued that "its strategic commitments exceed the resources available to support them." Calculating the savings of switching grand strategies, however, is not so simple, because it depends on the expenditures the current strategy demands and the amount required for its replacement—numbers that are hard to pin down.

If the United States revoked all its security guarantees, brought home all its troops, shrank every branch of the military, and slashed its nuclear arsenal, it would save around $900 billion over ten years, according to Benjamin Friedman and Justin Logan of the Cato Institute. But few advocates of retrenchment endorse such a radical reduction; instead, most call for "restraint," an "offshore balancing" strategy, or an "over the horizon" military posture. The savings these approaches would yield are less clear, since they depend on which security commitments Washington would abandon outright and how much it would cost to keep the remaining ones. If retrenchment simply meant shipping foreign-based U.S. forces back to the United States, then the savings would be modest at best, since the countries hosting U.S. forces usually cover a large portion of the basing costs. And if it meant maintaining a major expeditionary capacity, then any savings would again be small, since the Pentagon would still have to pay for the expensive weaponry and equipment required for projecting power abroad.

The other side of the cost equation, the price of continued engagement, is also in flux. Although the fat defense budgets of the past decade make an easy target for advocates of retrenchment, such high levels of spending aren't needed to maintain an engaged global posture. Spending skyrocketed after 9/11, but it has already begun to fall back to earth as the United States winds down its two costly wars and trims its base level of nonwar spending. As of the fall of 2012, the Defense Department was planning for cuts of just under $500 billion over the next five years, which it maintains will not compromise national security. These reductions would lower military spending to a little less than three percent of GDP by 2017, from its current level of 4.5 percent. The Pentagon could save even more with no ill effects by reforming its procurement practices and compensation policies.

Even without major budget cuts, however, the country can afford the costs of its ambitious grand strategy. The significant increases in military spending proposed by Mitt Romney, the Republican candidate, during the 2012 presidential campaign would still have kept military spending below its current share of GDP, since spending on the wars in Afghanistan and Iraq would still have gone down and Romney's proposed nonwar spending levels would not have kept pace with economic growth. Small wonder, then, that the case for pulling back rests more on the nonmonetary costs that the current strategy supposedly incurs.

UNBALANCED

One such alleged cost of the current grand strategy is that, in the words of the political scientist Barry Posen, it "prompts states to balance against U.S. power however they can." Yet there is no evidence that countries have banded together in anti-American alliances or tried to match the United States' military capacity on their own—or that they will do so in the future.

Indeed, it's hard to see how the current grand strategy could generate true counterbalancing. Unlike past hegemons, the United States is geographically isolated, which means that it is far less threatening to other major states and that it faces no contiguous great-power rivals that could step up to the task of balancing against it. Moreover, any competitor would have a hard time matching the U.S. military. Not only is the United States so far ahead militarily in both quantitative and qualitative terms, but its security guarantees also give it the leverage to prevent allies from giving military technology to potential U.S. rivals. Because the United States dominates the high-end defense industry, it can trade access to its defense market for allies' agreement not to transfer key military technologies to its competitors. The embargo that the United States has convinced the EU to maintain on military sales to China since 1989 is a case in point.

If U.S. global leadership were prompting balancing, then one would expect actual examples of pushback—especially during the administration of George W. Bush, who pursued a foreign policy that seemed particularly unilateral. Yet since the Soviet Union collapsed, no major powers have tried to balance against the United States by seeking to match its military might or by assembling a formidable alliance; the prospect is simply too daunting. Instead, they have resorted to what scholars call "soft balancing," using international institutions and norms to constrain Washington. Setting aside the fact that soft balancing is a slippery concept and difficult to distinguish from everyday diplomatic competition, it is wrong to say that the practice only harms the United States. Arguably, as the global leader, the United States benefits from employing soft-balancing-style leverage more than any other country. After all, today's rules and institutions came about under its auspices and largely reflect its interests, and so they are in fact tailor-made for soft balancing by the United States itself. In 2011, for example, Washington coordinated action with several Southeast Asian states to oppose Beijing's claims in the South China Sea by pointing to established international law and norms.

Another argument for retrenchment holds that the United States will fall prey to the same fate as past hegemons and accelerate its own decline. In order to keep its ambitious strategy in place, the logic goes, the country will have to divert resources away from more productive purposes—infrastructure, education, scientific research, and so on—that are necessary to keep its economy competitive. Allies, meanwhile, can get away with lower military expenditures and grow faster than they otherwise would.

The historical evidence for this phenomenon is thin; for the most part, past superpowers lost their leadership not because they pursued hegemony but because other major powers balanced against them—a prospect that is not in the cards today. (If anything, leading states can use their position to stave off their decline.) A bigger problem with the warnings against "imperial overstretch" is that there is no reason to believe that the pursuit of global leadership saps economic growth. Instead, most studies by economists find no clear relationship between military expenditures and economic decline.

To be sure, if the United States were a dramatic outlier and spent around a quarter of its GDP on defense, as the Soviet Union did in its last decades, its growth and competitiveness would suffer. But in 2012, even as it fought a war in Afghanistan and conducted counterterrorism operations around the globe, Washington spent just 4.5 percent of GDP on defense—a relatively small fraction, historically speaking. (From 1950 to 1990, that figure averaged 7.6 percent.) Recent economic difficulties might prompt Washington to reevaluate its defense budgets and international commitments, but that does not mean that those policies caused the downturn. And any money freed up from dropping global commitments would not necessarily be spent in ways that would help the U.S. economy.

Likewise, U.S. allies' economic growth rates have nothing to do with any security subsidies they receive from Washington. The contention that lower military expenditures facilitated the rise of Japan, West Germany, and other countries dependent on U.S. defense guarantees may have seemed plausible during the last bout of declinist anxiety, in the 1980s. But these states eventually stopped climbing up the global economic ranks as their per capita wealth approached U.S. levels—just as standard models of economic growth would predict. Over the past 20 years, the United States has maintained its lead in per capita GDP over its European allies and Japan, even as those countries' defense efforts have fallen further behind. Their failure to modernize their militaries has only served to entrench the United States' dominance.

LED NOT INTO TEMPTATION

The costs of U.S. foreign policy that matter most, of course, are human lives, and critics of an expansive grand strategy worry that the United States might get dragged into unnecessary wars. Securing smaller allies, they argue, emboldens those states to take risks they would not otherwise accept, pulling the superpower sponsor into costly conflicts—a classic moral hazard problem. Concerned about the reputational costs of failing to honor the country's alliance commitments, U.S. leaders might go to war even when no national interests are at stake.

History shows, however, that great powers anticipate the danger of entrapment and structure their agreements to protect themselves from it. It is nearly impossible to find a clear case of a smaller power luring a reluctant great power into war. For decades, World War I served as the canonical example of entangling alliances supposedly drawing great powers into a fight, but an outpouring of new historical research has overturned the conventional wisdom, revealing that the war was more the result of a conscious decision on Germany's part to try to dominate Europe than a case of alliance entrapment.

If anything, alliances reduce the risk of getting pulled into a conflict. In East Asia, the regional security agreements that Washington struck after World War II were designed, in the words of the political scientist Victor Cha, to "constrain anticommunist allies in the region that might engage in aggressive behavior against adversaries that could entrap the United States in an unwanted larger war." The same logic is now at play in the U.S.-Taiwanese relationship. After cross-strait tensions flared in the 1990s and the first decade of this century, U.S. officials grew concerned that their ambiguous support for Taiwan might expose them to the risk of entrapment. So the Bush administration adjusted its policy, clarifying that its goal was to not only deter China from an unprovoked attack but also deter Taiwan from unilateral moves toward independence.

For many advocates of retrenchment, the problem is that the mere possession of globe-girdling military capabilities supposedly inflates policymakers' conception of the national interest, so much so that every foreign problem begins to look like America's to solve. Critics also argue that the country's military superiority causes it to seek total solutions to security problems, as in Afghanistan and Iraq, that could be dealt with in less costly ways. Only a country that possessed such awesome military power and faced no serious geopolitical rival would fail to be satisfied with partial fixes, such as containment, and instead embark on wild schemes of democracy building, the argument goes.

Furthermore, they contend, the United States' outsized military creates a sense of obligation to do something with it even when no U.S. interests are at stake. As Madeleine Albright, then the U.S. ambassador to the un, famously asked Colin Powell, then chairman of the Joint Chiefs of Staff, when debating intervention in Bosnia in 1993, "What's the point of having this superb military you're always talking about if we can't use it?"

If the U.S. military scrapped its forces and shuttered its bases, then the country would no doubt eliminate the risk of entering needless wars, having tied itself to the mast like Ulysses. But if it instead merely moved its forces over the horizon, as is more commonly proposed by advocates of retrenchment, whatever temptations there were to intervene would not disappear. The bigger problem with the idea that a forward posture distorts conceptions of the national interest, however, is that it rests on just one case: Iraq. That war is an outlier in terms of both its high costs (it accounts for some two-thirds of the casualties and budget costs of all U.S. wars since 1990) and the degree to which the United States shouldered them alone. In the Persian Gulf War and the interventions in Bosnia, Kosovo, Afghanistan, and Libya, U.S. allies bore more of the burden, controlling for the size of their economies and populations.

Besides, the Iraq war was not an inevitable consequence of pursuing the United States' existing grand strategy; many scholars and policymakers who prefer an engaged America strongly opposed the war. Likewise, continuing the current grand strategy in no way condemns the United States to more wars like it. Consider how the country, after it lost in Vietnam, waged the rest of the Cold War with proxies and highly limited interventions. Iraq has generated a similar reluctance to undertake large expeditionary operations—what the political scientist John Mueller has dubbed "the Iraq syndrome." Those contending that the United States' grand strategy ineluctably leads the country into temptation need to present much more evidence before their case can be convincing.

KEEPING THE PEACE

Of course, even if it is true that the costs of deep engagement fall far below what advocates of retrenchment claim, they would not be worth bearing unless they yielded greater benefits. In fact, they do. The most obvious benefit of the current strategy is that it reduces the risk of a dangerous conflict. The United States' security commitments deter states with aspirations to regional hegemony from contemplating expansion and dissuade U.S. partners from trying to solve security problems on their own in ways that would end up threatening other states.

Skeptics discount this benefit by arguing that U.S. security guarantees aren't necessary to prevent dangerous rivalries from erupting. They maintain that the high costs of territorial conquest and the many tools countries can use to signal their benign intentions are enough to prevent conflict. In other words, major powers could peacefully manage regional multipolarity without the American pacifier.

But that outlook is too sanguine. If Washington got out of East Asia, Japan and South Korea would likely expand their military capabilities and go nuclear, which could provoke a destabilizing reaction from China. It's worth noting that during the Cold War, both South Korea and Taiwan tried to obtain nuclear weapons; the only thing that stopped them was the United States, which used its security commitments to restrain their nuclear temptations. Similarly, were the United States to leave the Middle East, the countries currently backed by Washington—notably, Israel, Egypt, and Saudi Arabia—might act in ways that would intensify the region's security dilemmas.

There would even be reason to worry about Europe. Although it's hard to imagine the return of great-power military competition in a post-American Europe, it's not difficult to foresee governments there refusing to pay the budgetary costs of higher military outlays and the political costs of increasing EU defense cooperation. The result might be a continent incapable of securing itself from threats on its periphery, unable to join foreign interventions on which U.S. leaders might want European help, and vulnerable to the influence of outside rising powers.

Given how easily a U.S. withdrawal from key regions could lead to dangerous competition, advocates of retrenchment tend to put forth another argument: that such rivalries wouldn't actually hurt the United States. To be sure, few doubt that the United States could survive the return of conflict among powers in Asia or the Middle East—but at what cost? Were states in one or both of these regions to start competing against one another, they would likely boost their military budgets, arm client states, and perhaps even start regional proxy wars, all of which should concern the United States, in part because its lead in military capabilities would narrow.

Greater regional insecurity could also produce cascades of nuclear proliferation as powers such as Egypt, Saudi Arabia, Japan, South Korea, and Taiwan built nuclear forces of their own. Those countries' regional competitors might then also seek nuclear arsenals. Although nuclear deterrence can promote stability between two states with the kinds of nuclear forces that the Soviet Union and the United States possessed, things get shakier when there are multiple nuclear rivals with less robust arsenals. As the number of nuclear powers increases, the probability of illicit transfers, irrational decisions, accidents, and unforeseen crises goes up.

The case for abandoning the United States' global role misses the underlying security logic of the current approach. By reassuring allies and actively managing regional relations, Washington dampens competition in the world's key areas, thereby preventing the emergence of a hothouse in which countries would grow new military capabilities. For proof that this strategy is working, one need look no further than the defense budgets of the current great powers: on average, since 1991 they have kept their military expenditures as a percentage of GDP to historic lows, and they have not attempted to match the United States' top-end military capabilities. Moreover, all of the world's most modern militaries are U.S. allies, and the United States' military lead over its potential rivals is by many measures growing.

On top of all this, the current grand strategy acts as a hedge against the emergence regional hegemons. Some supporters of retrenchment argue that the U.S. military should keep its forces over the horizon and pass the buck to local powers to do the dangerous work of counterbalancing rising regional powers. Washington, they contend, should deploy forces abroad only when a truly credible contender for regional hegemony arises, as in the cases of Germany and Japan during World War II and the Soviet Union during the Cold War. Yet there is already a potential contender for regional hegemony—China—and to balance it, the United States will need to maintain its key alliances in Asia and the military capacity to intervene there. The implication is that the United States should get out of Afghanistan and Iraq, reduce its military presence in Europe, and pivot to Asia. Yet that is exactly what the Obama administration is doing.

MILITARY DOMINANCE, ECONOMIC PREEMINENCE

Preoccupied with security issues, critics of the current grand strategy miss one of its most important benefits: sustaining an open global economy and a favorable place for the United States within it. To be sure, the sheer size of its output would guarantee the United States a major role in the global economy whatever grand strategy it adopted. Yet the country's military dominance undergirds its economic leadership. In addition to protecting the world economy from instability, its military commitments and naval superiority help secure the sea-lanes and other shipping corridors that allow trade to flow freely and cheaply. Were the United States to pull back from the world, the task of securing the global commons would get much harder. Washington would have less leverage with which it could convince countries to cooperate on economic matters and less access to the military bases throughout the world needed to keep the seas open.

A global role also lets the United States structure the world economy in ways that serve its particular economic interests. During the Cold War, Washington used its overseas security commitments to get allies to embrace the economic policies it preferred—convincing West Germany in the 1960s, for example, to take costly steps to support the U.S. dollar as a reserve currency. U.S. defense agreements work the same way today. For example, when negotiating the 2011 free-trade agreement with South Korea, U.S. officials took advantage of Seoul's desire to use the agreement as a means of tightening its security relations with Washington. As one diplomat explained to us privately, "We asked for changes in labor and environment clauses, in auto clauses, and the Koreans took it all." Why? Because they feared a failed agreement would be "a setback to the political and security relationship."

More broadly, the United States wields its security leverage to shape the overall structure of the global economy. Much of what the United States wants from the economic order is more of the same: for instance, it likes the current structure of the World Trade Organization and the International Monetary Fund and prefers that free trade continue. Washington wins when U.S. allies favor this status quo, and one reason they are inclined to support the existing system is because they value their military alliances. Japan, to name one example, has shown interest in the Trans-Pacific Partnership, the Obama administration's most important free-trade initiative in the region, less because its economic interests compel it to do so than because Prime Minister Yoshihiko Noda believes that his support will strengthen Japan's security ties with the United States.

The United States' geopolitical dominance also helps keep the U.S. dollar in place as the world's reserve currency, which confers enormous benefits on the country, such as a greater ability to borrow money. This is perhaps clearest with Europe: the EU's dependence on the United States for its security precludes the EU from having the kind of political leverage to support the euro that the United States has with the dollar. As with other aspects of the global economy, the United States does not provide its leadership for free: it extracts disproportionate gains. Shirking that responsibility would place those benefits at risk.

CREATING COOPERATION

What goes for the global economy goes for other forms of international cooperation. Here, too, American leadership benefits many countries but disproportionately helps the United States. In order to counter transnational threats, such as terrorism, piracy, organized crime, climate change, and pandemics, states have to work together and take collective action. But cooperation does not come about effortlessly, especially when national interests diverge. The United States' military efforts to promote stability and its broader leadership make it easier for Washington to launch joint initiatives and shape them in ways that reflect U.S. interests. After all, cooperation is hard to come by in regions where chaos reigns, and it flourishes where leaders can anticipate lasting stability.

U.S. alliances are about security first, but they also provide the political framework and channels of communication for cooperation on nonmilitary issues. NATO, for example, has spawned new institutions, such as the Atlantic Council, a think tank, that make it easier for Americans and Europeans to talk to one another and do business. Likewise, consultations with allies in East Asia spill over into other policy issues; for example, when American diplomats travel to Seoul to manage the military alliance, they also end up discussing the Trans-Pacific Partnership. Thanks to conduits such as this, the United States can use bargaining chips in one issue area to make progress in others.

The benefits of these communication channels are especially pronounced when it comes to fighting the kinds of threats that require new forms of cooperation, such as terrorism and pandemics. With its alliance system in place, the United States is in a stronger position than it would otherwise be to advance cooperation and share burdens. For example, the intelligence-sharing network within NATO, which was originally designed to gather information on the Soviet Union, has been adapted to deal with terrorism. Similarly, after a tsunami in the Indian Ocean devastated surrounding countries in 2004, Washington had a much easier time orchestrating a fast humanitarian response with Australia, India, and Japan, since their militaries were already comfortable working with one another. The operation did wonders for the United States' image in the region.

The United States' global role also has the more direct effect of facilitating the bargains among governments that get cooperation going in the first place. As the scholar Joseph Nye has written, "The American military role in deterring threats to allies, or of assuring access to a crucial resource such as oil in the Persian Gulf, means that the provision of protective force can be used in bargaining situations. Sometimes the linkage may be direct; more often it is a factor not mentioned openly but present in the back of statesmen's minds."

THE DEVIL WE KNOW

Should America come home? For many prominent scholars of international relations, the answer is yes—a view that seems even wiser in the wake of the disaster in Iraq and the Great Recession. Yet their arguments simply don't hold up. There is little evidence that the United States would save much money switching to a smaller global posture. Nor is the current strategy self-defeating: it has not provoked the formation of counterbalancing coalitions or caused the country to spend itself into economic decline. Nor will it condemn the United States to foolhardy wars in the future. What the strategy does do is help prevent the outbreak of conflict in the world's most important regions, keep the global economy humming, and make international cooperation easier. Charting a different course would threaten all these benefits.

This is not to say that the United States' current foreign policy can't be adapted to new circumstances and challenges. Washington does not need to retain every commitment at all costs, and there is nothing wrong with rejiggering its strategy in response to new opportunities or setbacks. That is what the Nixon administration did by winding down the Vietnam War and increasing the United States' reliance on regional partners to contain Soviet power, and it is what the Obama administration has been doing after the Iraq war by pivoting to Asia. These episodes of rebalancing belie the argument that a powerful and internationally engaged America cannot tailor its policies to a changing world.

A grand strategy of actively managing global security and promoting the liberal economic order has served the United States exceptionally well for the past six decades, and there is no reason to give it up now. The country's globe-spanning posture is the devil we know, and a world with a disengaged America is the devil we don't know. Were American leaders to choose retrenchment, they would in essence be running a massive experiment to test how the world would work without an engaged and liberal leading power. The results could well be disastrous.

Pull Back

The Case for a Less Activist Foreign Policy

Barry R. Posen

Despite a decade of costly and indecisive warfare and mounting fiscal pressures, the long-standing consensus among American policymakers about U.S. grand strategy has remained remarkably intact. As the presidential campaign made clear, Republicans and Democrats may quibble over foreign policy at the margins, but they agree on the big picture: that the United States should dominate the world militarily, economically, and politically, as it has since the final years of the Cold War, a strategy of liberal hegemony. The country, they hold, needs to preserve its massive lead in the global balance of power, consolidate its economic preeminence, enlarge the community of market democracies, and maintain its outsized influence in the international institutions it helped create.

To this end, the U.S. government has expanded its sprawling Cold War-era network of security commitments and military bases. It has reinforced its existing alliances, adding new members to NATO and enhancing its security agreement with Japan. In the Persian Gulf, it has sought to protect the flow of oil with a full panoply of air, sea, and land forces, a goal that consumes at least 15 percent of the U.S. defense budget. Washington has put China on

BARRY R. POSEN is Ford International Professor of Political Science and Director of the Security Studies Program at the Massachusetts Institute of Technology.

a watch list, ringing it in with a network of alliances, less formal relationships, and military bases.

The United States' activism has entailed a long list of ambitious foreign policy projects. Washington has tried to rescue failing states, intervening militarily in Somalia, Haiti, Bosnia, Kosovo, and Libya, variously attempting to defend human rights, suppress undesirable nationalist movements, and install democratic regimes. It has also tried to contain so-called rogue states that oppose the United States, such as Iran, Iraq under Saddam Hussein, North Korea, and, to a lesser degree, Syria. After 9/11, the struggle against al Qaeda and its allies dominated the agenda, but the George W. Bush administration defined this enterprise broadly and led the country into the painful wars in Afghanistan and Iraq. Although the United States has long sought to discourage the spread of nuclear weapons, the prospect of nuclear-armed terrorists has added urgency to this objective, leading to constant tension with Iran and North Korea.

In pursuit of this ambitious agenda, the United States has consistently spent hundreds of billions of dollars per year on its military—far more than the sum of the defense budgets of its friends and far more than the sum of those of its potential adversaries. It has kept that military busy: U.S. troops have spent roughly twice as many months in combat after the Cold War as they did during it. Today, roughly 180,000 U.S. soldiers remain stationed on foreign soil, not counting the tens of thousands more who have rotated through the war zones in Afghanistan and Iraq. Thousands of American and allied soldiers have lost their lives, not to mention the countless civilians caught in the crossfire.

This undisciplined, expensive, and bloody strategy has done untold harm to U.S. national security. It makes enemies almost as fast as it slays them, discourages allies from paying for their own defense, and convinces powerful states to band together and oppose Washington's plans, further raising the costs of carrying out its foreign policy. During the 1990s, these consequences were manageable because the United States enjoyed such a favorable power position and chose its wars carefully. Over the last decade, however, the country's relative power has deteriorated, and policymakers have made dreadful choices concerning which wars to fight and how to fight them. What's more, the Pentagon has come to depend on continuous infusions of cash simply to retain its current force structure—levels of spending that the Great Recession and the United States' ballooning debt have rendered unsustainable.

It is time to abandon the United States' hegemonic strategy and replace it with one of restraint. This approach would mean giving up on global reform and sticking to protecting narrow national security interests. It would mean transforming the military into a smaller force that goes to war only when it truly must. It would mean removing large numbers of U.S. troops from forward bases, creating incentives for allies to provide for their own security. And because such a shift would allow the United States to spend its resources on only the most pressing international threats, it would help preserve the country's prosperity and security over the long run.

ACTION AND REACTION

The United States emerged from the Cold War as the single most powerful state in modern times, a position that its diversified and immensely productive economy supports. Although its share of world economic output will inevitably shrink as other countries catch up, the United States will continue for many years to rank as one of the top two or three economies in the world. The United States' per capita GDP stands at $48,000, more than five times as large as China's, which means that the U.S. economy can produce cutting-edge products for a steady domestic market. North America is blessed with enviable quantities of raw materials, and about 29 percent of U.S. trade flows to and from its immediate neighbors, Canada and Mexico. The fortuitous geostrategic position of the United States compounds these economic advantages. Its neighbors to the north and south possess only miniscule militaries. Vast oceans to the west and east separate it from potential rivals.

And its thousands of nuclear weapons deter other countries from ever entertaining an invasion.

Ironically, however, instead of relying on these inherent advantages for its security, the United States has acted with a profound sense of insecurity, adopting an unnecessarily militarized and forward-leaning foreign policy. That strategy has generated predictable pushback. Since the 1990s, rivals have resorted to what scholars call "soft balancing"—low-grade diplomatic opposition. China and Russia regularly use the rules of liberal international institutions to delegitimize the United States' actions. In the UN Security Council, they wielded their veto power to deny the West resolutions supporting the bombing campaign in Kosovo in 1999 and the invasion of Iraq in 2003, and more recently, they have slowed the effort to isolate Syria. They occasionally work together in other venues, too, such as the Shanghai Cooperation Organization. Although the Beijing-Moscow relationship is unimpressive compared with military alliances such as NATO, it's remarkable that it exists at all given the long history of border friction and hostility between the two countries. As has happened so often in history, the common threat posed by a greater power has driven unnatural partners to cooperate.

American activism has also generated harder forms of balancing. China has worked assiduously to improve its military, and Russia has sold it modern weapons, such as fighter aircraft, surface-to-air missiles, and diesel-electric submarines. Iran and North Korea, meanwhile, have pursued nuclear programs in part to neutralize the United States' overwhelming advantages in conventional fighting power. Some of this pushback would have occurred no matter what; in an anarchic global system, states acquire the allies and military power that help them look after themselves. But a country as large and as active as the United States intensifies these responses.

Such reactions will only grow stronger as emerging economies convert their wealth into military power. Even though the economic and technological capacities of China and India may never equal those of the United States, the gap is destined to narrow.

China already has the potential to be a serious competitor. At the peak of the Cold War, in the mid-1970s, Soviet GDP, in terms of purchasing power parity, amounted to 57 percent of U.S. GDP. China reached 75 percent of the U.S. level in 2011, and according to the International Monetary Fund, it is projected to match it by 2017. Of course, Chinese output must support four times as many people, which limits what the country can extract for military purposes, but it still provides enough resources to hinder U.S. foreign policy. Meanwhile, Russia, although a shadow of its former Soviet self, is no longer the hapless weakling it was in the 1990s. Its economy is roughly the size of the United Kingdom's or France's, it has plenty of energy resources to export, and it still produces some impressive weapons systems.

FIGHTING IDENTITY

Just as emerging powers have gotten stronger, so, too, have the small states and violent substate entities that the United States has attempted to discipline, democratize, or eliminate. Whether in Somalia, Serbia, Afghanistan, Iraq, or Libya, the U.S. military seems to find itself fighting enemies that prove tougher than expected. (Consider the fact that Washington spent as much in real terms on the war in Iraq as it did on the war in Vietnam, even though the Iraqi insurgents enjoyed little external support, whereas China and the Soviet Union lent major support to the Vietcong and the North Vietnamese.) Yet Washington seems unable to stay out of conflicts involving substate entities, in part because their elemental nature assaults the internationalist values that U.S. grand strategy is committed to preserving. Having trumpeted the United States' military superiority, U.S. policymakers have a hard time saying no to those who argue that the country's prestige will suffer gravely if the world's leader lets wars great and small run their course.

The enduring strength of these substate groups should give American policymakers pause, since the United States' current grand strategy entails open-ended confrontation with nationalism and other forms of identity politics that insurgents and terrorists feed off of. These forces provide the organizing energy for groups competing for power within countries (as in Bosnia, Afghanistan, and Iraq), for secessionist movements (as in Kosovo), and for terrorists who oppose the liberal world order (mainly al Qaeda). Officials in Washington, however, have acted as if they can easily undercut the power of identity through democratic processes, freedom of information, and economic development, helped along by the judicious application of military power. In fact, identity is resilient, and foreign peoples react with hostility to outsiders trying to control their lives.

The Iraq war has been a costly case in point. Officials in the Bush administration convinced themselves that a quick application of overwhelming military power would bring democracy to Iraq, produce a subsequent wave of democratization across the Arab world, marginalize al Qaeda, and secure U.S. influence in the region. Instead, Shiites, Sunnis, and Kurds stoked the violence that the United States labored to suppress, and Shiite and Sunni factions fought not only each other but also the U.S. military. Today's Shiite-dominated government in Baghdad has proved neither democratic nor effective. Sunni terrorists have continued to carry out attacks. The Kurdish parts of Iraq barely acknowledge their membership in the larger state.

By now, it is clear that the United States has worn out its welcome in Afghanistan, too. The Taliban continue to resist the U.S. presence, drawing their strength largely from Pashtun nationalism, and members of the Afghan security forces have, in growing numbers, murdered U.S. and other NATO soldiers who were there to assist them. Instead of simply punishing the Taliban for their indirect role in 9/11 and hitting al Qaeda as hard as possible, true to its global agenda, the Bush administration pursued a costly and futile effort to transform Afghanistan, and the Obama administration continued it.

FRIENDS WITHOUT BENEFITS

Another problematic response to the United States' grand strategy comes from its friends: free-riding. The Cold War alliances that the country has worked so hard to maintain—namely, NATO and the U.S.-Japanese security agreement—have provided U.S. partners in Europe and Asia with such a high level of insurance that they have been able to steadily shrink their militaries and outsource their defense to Washington. European nations have cut their military spending by roughly 15 percent in real terms since the end of the Cold War, with the exception of the United Kingdom, which will soon join the rest as it carries out its austerity policy. Depending on how one counts, Japanese defense spending has been cut, or at best has remained stable, over the past decade. The government has unwisely devoted too much spending to ground forces, even as its leaders have expressed alarm at the rise of Chinese military power—an air, missile, and naval threat.

Although these regions have avoided major wars, the United States has had to bear more and more of the burden of keeping the peace. It now spends 4.6 percent of its GDP on defense, whereas its European NATO allies collectively spend 1.6 percent and Japan spends 1.0 percent. With their high per capita GDPs, these allies can afford to devote more money to their militaries, yet they have no incentive to do so. And so while the U.S. government considers draconian cuts in social spending to restore the United States' fiscal health, it continues to subsidize the security of Germany and Japan. This is welfare for the rich.

U.S. security guarantees also encourage plucky allies to challenge more powerful states, confident that Washington will save them in the end—a classic case of moral hazard. This phenomenon has caused the United States to incur political costs, antagonizing powers great and small for no gain and encouraging them to seek opportunities to provoke the United States in return. So far, the United States has escaped getting sucked into unnecessary wars, although Washington dodged a bullet in Taiwan when the Democratic Progressive Party of Chen Shui-bian governed the island, from 2000 to 2008. His frequent allusions to independence, which ran counter to U.S. policy but which some Bush administration officials reportedly encouraged, unnecessarily provoked the Chinese government; had he proceeded, he would have surely triggered a dangerous crisis. Chen would never have entertained such reckless rhetoric absent the long-standing backing of the U.S. government.

The Philippines and Vietnam (the latter of which has no formal defense treaty with Washington) also seem to have figured out that they can needle China over maritime boundary disputes and then seek shelter under the U.S. umbrella when China inevitably reacts. Not only do these disputes make it harder for Washington to cooperate with Beijing on issues of global importance; they also risk roping the United States into conflicts over strategically marginal territory.

Georgia is another state that has played this game to the United States' detriment. Overly confident of Washington's affection for it, the tiny republic deliberately challenged Russia over control of the disputed region of South Ossetia in August 2008. Regardless of how exactly the fighting began, Georgia acted far too adventurously given its size, proximity to Russia, and distance from any plausible source of military help. This needless war ironically made Russia look tough and the United States unreliable.

This dynamic is at play in the Middle East, too. Although U.S. officials have communicated time and again to leaders in Jerusalem their discomfort with Israeli settlements on the territory occupied during the 1967 war, Israel regularly increases the population and dimensions of those settlements. The United States' military largess and regular affirmations of support for Israel have convinced Israeli hawks that they will suffer no consequences for ignoring U.S. advice. It takes two to make peace in the Israeli-Palestinian conflict, but the creation of humiliating facts on the ground will not bring a negotiated settlement any closer. And Israel's policies toward the Palestinians are a serious impediment to improved U.S. relations with the Arab world.

A NIMBLER STRATEGY

The United States should replace its unnecessary, ineffective, and expensive hegemonic quest with a more restrained grand strategy.

Washington should not retreat into isolationism but refocus its efforts on its three biggest security challenges: preventing a powerful rival from upending the global balance of power, fighting terrorists, and limiting nuclear proliferation. These challenges are not new, but the United States must develop more carefully calculated and discriminating policies to address them.

For roughly a century, American strategists have striven to ensure that no single state dominated the giant landmass of Eurasia, since such a power could then muster the resources to threaten the United States directly. To prevent this outcome, the United States rightly went to war against Germany and Japan and contained the Soviet Union. Although China may ultimately try to assume the mantle of Eurasian hegemon, this outcome is neither imminent nor inevitable. China's economy still faces many pitfalls, and the country is surrounded by powerful states that could and would check its expansion, including India and Russia, both of which have nuclear weapons. Japan, although it underspends on defense today, is rich and technologically advanced enough to contribute to a coalition of states that could balance against China. Other maritime Asian countries, even without the United States as a backstop, could also make common cause against China. The United States should maintain the capability to assist them if need be. But it should proceed cautiously in order to ensure that its efforts do not unnecessarily threaten China and thus encourage the very ambitions Washington hopes to deter or prompt a new round of free-riding or reckless driving by others in Asia.

The United States must also defend itself against al Qaeda and any similar successor groups. Since such terrorists can threaten Americans' lives, the U.S. government should keep in place the prudent defensive measures that have helped lower the risk of attacks, such as more energetic intelligence efforts and better airport security. (A less interventionist foreign policy will help, too: it was partly the U.S. military's presence in Saudi Arabia that radicalized Osama bin Laden and his followers in the first place.) When it comes to offense, the United States must still pursue terrorists operating abroad, so that they spend their scarce resources trying to stay alive rather than plotting new attacks. It will need to continue cooperating with other vulnerable governments and help them develop their own police and military forces. Occasionally, the U.S. military will have to supplement these efforts with air strikes, drone attacks, and special operations raids.

But Washington should keep the threat in perspective. Terrorists are too weak to threaten the country's sovereignty, territorial integrity, or power position. Because the threat is modest, and because trying to reform other societies by force is too costly, the United States must fight terrorism with carefully applied force, rather than through wholesale nation-building efforts such as that in Afghanistan.

Finally, a restrained grand strategy would also pay close attention to the spread of nuclear weapons, while relying less on the threat of military force to stop it. Thanks to the deterrence provided by its own massive nuclear forces, the United States faces little risk of a direct nuclear attack by another state. But Washington does need to keep nonstate actors from obtaining nuclear weapons or material. To prevent them from taking advantage of lax safeguards at nuclear facilities, the U.S. government should share best practices regarding nuclear security with other countries, even ones that it would prefer did not possess nuclear weapons in the first place. The United States does already cooperate somewhat with Pakistan on this issue, but it must stand ready to do more and ultimately to undertake such efforts with others.

The loss of a government's control over its nuclear weapons during a coup, revolution, or civil war is a far harder problem to forestall. It may be possible for U.S. forces to secure weapons in a period of instability, with the help of local actors who see the dangers for their own country if the weapons get loose. Conditions may lend themselves to a preventive military attack, to seize or disable the weapons. In some cases, however, the United States might have to make do with less sure-fire responses. It could warn those who seized the nuclear weapons in a period of upheaval that they would make themselves targets for retaliation if the weapons were ever used by terrorists. And it could better surveil international sea and air routes and more intensively monitor both its own borders for nuclear smuggling and those of the potential source countries.

These measures may seem incommensurate with the terrible toll of a nuclear blast. But the alternative strategy—fighting preventive conventional wars against nascent nuclear powers—is an expensive and uncertain solution to proliferation. The Obama administration's oft-repeated warning that deterrence and containment of a nuclear Iran is unacceptable makes little sense given the many ways a preventive war could go wrong and in light of the redundant deterrent capability the United States already possesses. Indeed, the more Washington relies on military force to halt proliferation, the more likely it is that countries will decide to acquire the ultimate deterrent.

A more restrained America would also have to head off nuclear arms races. In retrospect, the size, composition, doctrine, and highly alert posture of U.S. and Soviet nuclear forces during the Cold War seem unduly risky relative to the strategic problem those weapons were supposed to solve. Nuclear weapons act as potent deterrents to aggression, but significantly smaller forces than those the United States now possesses, carefully managed, should do the job. To avoid a replay of Cold War-style nuclear competition, the United States should pursue a new multilateral arms control regime that places ceilings on nuclear inventories and avoids hair-trigger force postures.

RESTRAINT IN PRACTICE

A grand strategy of restraint would narrow U.S. foreign policy to focus on those three larger objectives. What would it look like in practice? First, the United States would recast its alliances so that other countries shared actual responsibility for their own defense. NATO is the easiest case; the United States should withdraw from the military command structure and return the alliance to the primarily political organization it once was. The Europeans can decide for themselves whether they want to retain the military command structure under the auspices of the European Union or dismantle it altogether. Most U.S. troops should come home from Europe, although by mutual agreement, the United States could keep a small number of naval and air bases on the continent.

The security treaty with Japan is a more difficult problem; it needs to be renegotiated but not abandoned. As the treaty stands now, the United States shoulders most of the burden of defending Japan, and the Japanese government agrees to help. The roles should be reversed, so that Japan assumes responsibility for its own defense, with Washington offering backup. Given concerns about China's rising power, not all U.S. forces should leave the region. But the Pentagon should pare down its presence in Japan to those relevant to the most immediate military problems. All U.S. marines could be withdrawn from the country, bringing to an end the thorny negotiations about their future on the island of Okinawa. The U.S. Navy and the U.S. Air Force should keep the bulk of their forces stationed in and around Japan in place, but with appropriate reductions. Elsewhere in Asia, the U.S. military can cooperate with other states to ensure access to the region should future crises arise, but it should not seek new permanent bases.

The military should also reassess its commitments in the Persian Gulf: the United States should help protect states in the region against external attacks, but it cannot take responsibility for defending them against internal dissent. Washington still needs to reassure those governments that fear that a regional power such as Iran will attack them and hijack their oil wealth, since a single oil-rich hegemon in the region would no doubt be a source of mischief. The U.S. military has proved adept at preventing such an outcome in the past, as it did when it defended Saudi Arabia and repelled Saddam's forces from Kuwait in 1991. Ground forces bent on invasion make easy targets for air attacks. The aircraft and cruise missiles aboard U.S. naval forces stationed in the region could provide immediate assistance. With a little advance notice, U.S. Air Force aircraft could quickly reinforce land bases maintained by the Arab states of the Gulf, as they did during the Gulf War when the regional powers opposed to Saddam's aggression prepared the way for reinforcement from the U.S. military by maintaining extra base capacity and fuel.

But U.S. soldiers no longer need to live onshore in Gulf countries, where they incite anti-Americanism and tie the U.S. government to autocratic regimes of dubious legitimacy. For example, Bahrain is suffering considerable internal unrest, which raises questions about the future viability of the United States' growing military presence there. The Iraq war proved that trying to install new regimes in Arab countries is a fool's errand; defending existing regimes facing internal rebellion will be no easier.

Under a restrained grand strategy, U.S. military forces could shrink significantly, both to save money and to send allies the message that it's time they did more for themselves. Because the Pentagon would, under this new strategy, swear off counterinsurgency, it could cut the number of ground forces in half. The navy and the air force, meanwhile, should be cut by only a quarter to a third, since their assets take a long time to produce and would still be needed for any effort to maintain the global balance of power. Naval and air forces are also well suited to solving the security problems of Asia and the Persian Gulf. Because these forces are highly mobile, only some need be present in key regions. The rest can be kept at home, as a powerful strategic reserve.

The overall size and quality of U.S. military forces should be determined by the critical contingency that they must address: the defense of key resources and allies against direct attack. Too often in the past, Washington has overused its expensive military to send messages that ought to be left to diplomats. That must change. Although the Pentagon should continue leading joint exercises with the militaries of other countries in key regions, it should stop overloading the calendar with pointless exercises the world over. Making that change would save wear and tear on troops and equipment and avoid creating the impression that the United States will solve all the world's security problems.

LETTING GO

Shifting to a more restrained global stance would yield meaningful benefits for the United States, saving lives and resources and preventing pushback, provided Washington makes deliberate and prudent moves now to prepare its allies to take on the responsibility for their own defense. Scaling down the U.S. military's presence over a decade would give partners plenty of time to fortify their own militaries and develop the political and diplomatic machinery to look after their own affairs. Gradual disengagement would also reduce the chances of creating security vacuums, which opportunistic regional powers might try to fill.

U.S. allies, of course, will do everything they can to persuade Washington to keep its current policies in place. Some will promise improvements to their military forces that they will then abandon when it is convenient. Some will claim there is nothing more they can contribute, that their domestic political and economic constraints matter more than America's. Others will try to divert the discussion to shared values and principles. Still others will hint that they will bandwagon with strong neighbors rather than balance against them. A few may even threaten to turn belligerent.

U.S. policymakers will need to remain cool in the face of such tactics and keep in mind that these wealthy allies are unlikely to surrender their sovereignty to regional powers. Indeed, history has shown that states more often balance against the powerful than bandwagon with them. As for potential adversaries, the United States can continue to deter actions that threaten its vital interests by defining those interests narrowly, stating them clearly, and maintaining enough military power to protect them.

Of course, the United States could do none of these things and instead continue on its present track, wasting resources and earning the enmity of some states and peoples while infantilizing others. Perhaps current economic and geopolitical trends will reverse themselves, and the existing strategy will leave Washington comfortably in the driver's seat, with others eager to live according to its rules. But if the U.S. debt keeps growing and power continues to shift to other countries, some future economic or political crisis could force Washington to switch course abruptly, compelling friendly and not-so-friendly countries to adapt suddenly. That seems like the more dangerous path.

Why Iran Should Get the Bomb

Nuclear Balancing Would Mean Stability

Kenneth N. Waltz

The past several months have witnessed a heated debate over the best way for the United States and Israel to respond to Iran's nuclear activities. As the argument has raged, the United States has tightened its already robust sanctions regime against the Islamic Republic, and the European Union announced in January that it will begin an embargo on Iranian oil on July 1. Although the United States, the EU, and Iran have recently returned to the negotiating table, a palpable sense of crisis still looms.

It should not. Most U.S., European, and Israeli commentators and policymakers warn that a nuclear-armed Iran would be the worst possible outcome of the current standoff. In fact, it would probably be the best possible result: the one most likely to restore stability to the Middle East.

POWER BEGS TO BE BALANCED

The crisis over Iran's nuclear program could end in three different ways. First, diplomacy coupled with serious sanctions could convince Iran to abandon its pursuit of a nuclear weapon. But this outcome is unlikely: the historical record indicates that a country

KENNETH N. WALTZ is Senior Research Scholar at the Saltzman Institute of War and Peace Studies.

bent on acquiring nuclear weapons can rarely be dissuaded from doing so. Punishing a state through economic sanctions does not inexorably derail its nuclear program. Take North Korea, which succeeded in building its weapons despite countless roundsof sanctions and UN Security Council resolutions. If Tehran determines that its security depends on possessing nuclear weapons, sanctions are unlikely to change its mind. In fact, adding still more sanctions now could make Iran feel even more vulnerable, giving it still more reason to seek the protection of the ultimate deterrent.

The second possible outcome is that Iran stops short of testing a nuclear weapon but develops a breakout capability, the capacity to build and test one quite quickly. Iran would not be the first country to acquire a sophisticated nuclear program without building an actual bomb. Japan, for instance, maintains a vast civilian nuclear infrastructure. Experts believe that it could produce a nuclear weapon on short notice.

Such a breakout capability might satisfy the domestic political needs of Iran's rulers by assuring hard-liners that they can enjoy all the benefits of having a bomb (such as greater security) without the downsides (such as international isolation and condemnation). The problem is that a breakout capability might not work as intended.

The United States and its European allies are primarily concerned with weaponization, so they might accept a scenario in which Iran stops short of a nuclear weapon. Israel, however, has made it clear that it views a significant Iranian enrichment capacity alone as an unacceptable threat. It is possible, then, that a verifiable commitment from Iran to stop short of a weapon could appease major Western powers but leave the Israelis unsatisfied. Israel would be less intimidated by a virtual nuclear weapon than it would be by an actual one and therefore would likely continue its risky efforts at subverting Iran's nuclear program through sabotage and assassination—which could lead Iran to conclude that a breakout capability is an insufficient deterrent, after all, and that only weaponization can provide it with the security it seeks.

The third possible outcome of the standoff is that Iran continues its current course and publicly goes nuclear by testing a weapon. U.S. and Israeli officials have declared that outcome unacceptable, arguing that a nuclear Iran is a uniquely terrifying prospect, even an existential threat. Such language is typical of major powers, which have historically gotten riled up whenever another country has begun to develop a nuclear weapon of its own. Yet so far, every time another country has managed to shoulder its way into the nuclear club, the other members have always changed tack and decided to live with it. In fact, by reducing imbalances in military power, new nuclear states generally produce more regional and international stability, not less.

Israel's regional nuclear monopoly, which has proved remarkably durable for the past four decades, has long fueled instability in the Middle East. In no other region of the world does a lone, unchecked nuclear state exist. It is Israel's nuclear arsenal, not Iran's desire for one, that has contributed most to the current crisis. Power, after all, begs to be balanced. What is surprising about the Israeli case is that it has taken so long for a potential balancer to emerge.

Of course, it is easy to understand why Israel wants to remain the sole nuclear power in the region and why it is willing to use force to secure that status. In 1981, Israel bombed Iraq to prevent a challenge to its nuclear monopoly. It did the same to Syria in 2007 and is now considering similar action against Iran. But the very acts that have allowed Israel to maintain its nuclear edge in the short term have prolonged an imbalance that is unsustainable in the long term. Israel's proven ability to strike potential nuclear rivals with impunity has inevitably made its enemies anxious to develop the means to prevent Israel from doing so again. In this way, the current tensions are best viewed not as the early stages of a relatively recent Iranian nuclear crisis but rather as the final stages of a decades-long Middle East nuclear crisis that will end only when a balance of military power is restored.

UNFOUNDED FEARS

One reason the danger of a nuclear Iran has been grossly exaggerated is that the debate surrounding it has been distorted by misplaced worries and fundamental misunderstandings of how states generally behave in the international system. The first prominent concern, which undergirds many others, is that the Iranian regime is innately irrational. Despite a widespread belief to the contrary, Iranian policy is made not by "mad mullahs" but by perfectly sane ayatollahs who want to survive just like any other leaders. Although Iran's leaders indulge in inflammatory and hateful rhetoric, they show no propensity for self-destruction. It would be a grave error for policymakers in the United States and Israel to assume otherwise.

Yet that is precisely what many U.S. and Israeli officials and analysts have done. Portraying Iran as irrational has allowed them to argue that the logic of nuclear deterrence does not apply to the Islamic Republic. If Iran acquired a nuclear weapon, they warn, it would not hesitate to use it in a first strike against Israel, even though doing so would invite massive retaliation and risk destroying everything the Iranian regime holds dear.

Although it is impossible to be certain of Iranian intentions, it is far more likely that if Iran desires nuclear weapons, it is for the purpose of providing for its own security, not to improve its offensive capabilities (or destroy itself). Iran may be intransigent at the negotiating table and defiant in the face of sanctions, but it still acts to secure its own preservation. Iran's leaders did not, for example, attempt to close the Strait of Hormuz despite issuing blustery warnings that they might do so after the EU announced its planned oil embargo in January. The Iranian regime clearly concluded that it did not want to provoke what would surely have been a swift and devastating American response to such a move.

Nevertheless, even some observers and policymakers who accept that the Iranian regime is rational still worry that a nuclear weapon would embolden it, providing Tehran with a shield that would allow it to act more aggressively and increase its support for terrorism. Some analysts even fear that Iran would directly provide terrorists with nuclear arms. The problem with these concerns is that they contradict the record of every other nuclear weapons state going back to 1945. History shows that when countries acquire the bomb, they feel increasingly vulnerable and become acutely aware that their nuclear weapons make them a potential target in the eyes of major powers. This awareness discourages nuclear states from bold and aggressive action. Maoist China, for example, became much less bellicose after acquiring nuclear weapons in 1964, and India and Pakistan have both become more cautious since going nuclear. There is little reason to believe Iran would break this mold.

As for the risk of a handoff to terrorists, no country could transfer nuclear weapons without running a high risk of being found out. U.S. surveillance capabilities would pose a serious obstacle, as would the United States' impressive and growing ability to identify the source of fissile material. Moreover, countries can never entirely control or even predict the behavior of the terrorist groups they sponsor. Once a country such as Iran acquires a nuclear capability, it will have every reason to maintain full control over its arsenal. After all, building a bomb is costly and dangerous. It would make little sense to transfer the product of that investment to parties that cannot be trusted or managed.

Another oft-touted worry is that if Iran obtains the bomb, other states in the region will follow suit, leading to a nuclear arms race in the Middle East. But the nuclear age is now almost 70 years old, and so far, fears of proliferation have proved to be unfounded. Properly defined, the term "proliferation" means a rapid and uncontrolled spread. Nothing like that has occurred; in fact, since 1970, there has been a marked slowdown in the emergence of nuclear states. There is no reason to expect that this pattern will change now. Should Iran become the second Middle Eastern nuclear power since 1945, it would hardly signal the start of a landslide. When Israel acquired the bomb in the 1960s, it was at war with many of its neighbors. Its nuclear arms were a much bigger threat to the Arab world than Iran's program is today. If an atomic

Israel did not trigger an arms race then, there is no reason a nuclear Iran should now.

REST ASSURED

In 1991, the historical rivals India and Pakistan signed a treaty agreeing not to target each other's nuclear facilities. They realized that far more worrisome than their adversary's nuclear deterrent was the instability produced by challenges to it. Since then, even in the face of high tensions and risky provocations, the two countries have kept the peace. Israel and Iran would do well to consider this precedent. If Iran goes nuclear, Israel and Iran will deter each other, as nuclear powers always have. There has never been a full-scale war between two nuclear-armed states. Once Iran crosses the nuclear threshold, deterrence will apply, even if the Iranian arsenal is relatively small. No other country in the region will have an incentive to acquire its own nuclear capability, and the current crisis will finally dissipate, leading to a Middle East that is more stable than it is today.

For that reason, the United States and its allies need not take such pains to prevent the Iranians from developing a nuclear weapon. Diplomacy between Iran and the major powers should continue, because open lines of communication will make the Western countries feel better able to live with a nuclear Iran. But the current sanctions on Iran can be dropped: they primarily harm ordinary Iranians, with little purpose.

Most important, policymakers and citizens in the Arab world, Europe, Israel, and the United States should take comfort from the fact that history has shown that where nuclear capabilities emerge, so, too, does stability. When it comes to nuclear weapons, now as ever, more may be better.

Getting to Yes With Iran

The Challenges of Coercive Diplomacy

Robert Jervis

It might be wise for the United States to resign itself to Iran's development of nuclear weapons and to focus on deterring the Islamic Republic from ever using them. But U.S. leaders have explicitly rejected that course of action. "Make no mistake: a nuclear-armed Iran is not a challenge that can be contained," U.S. President Barack Obama told the UN General Assembly last September. "And that's why the United States will do what we must to prevent Iran from obtaining a nuclear weapon." U.S. officials have also made it clear that they consider direct military action to prevent Iran from acquiring a nuclear weapon an extremely unattractive option, one to be implemented only as a regrettable last resort.

In practice, then, that leaves only two tools for dealing with Iran's advancing nuclear program: threats and promises, the melding of which the political scientist Alexander George labeled "coercive diplomacy." To succeed in halting Iran's progress toward a bomb, the United States will have to combine the two, not simply alternate between them. It must make credible promises and credible threats simultaneously—an exceedingly difficult trick to pull

ROBERT JERVIS is Adlai E. Stevenson Professor of International Politics at Columbia University and a member of the Saltzman Institute of War and Peace Studies.

off. And in this particular case, the difficulty is compounded by a number of other factors: the long history of intense mutual mistrust between the two countries; the U.S. alliance with Iran's arch-enemy, Israel; and the opacity of Iranian decision-making.

The odds of overcoming all these obstacles are long. If Washington truly wants to avoid both deterrence and military action, therefore, it will need to up its game and take an unusually smart and bold approach to negotiations.

WHY COERCIVE DIPLOMACY IS HARD

The United States' recent record of coercive diplomacy is not encouraging. A combination of sanctions, inspections, and threats led Iraqi President Saddam Hussein to freeze his weapons of mass destruction program after the Gulf War, but it did not coerce him into accepting a long-term agreement. The reasons, as researchers have learned since Saddam's ouster, had to do with his motives and perceptions. The Iraqi leader not only sought regional dominance and the destruction of Israel but also worried about appearing weak to Iran, saw his survival in the wake of the Gulf War as a victory, and was so suspicious of the United States that a real rapprochement was never within reach. All this rendered ineffective the threats issued by the George W. Bush administration during the run-up to the 2003 U.S. invasion of Iraq and would likely have made promises of a reasonable settlement ineffective as well.

The Iraq case, moreover, is less an exception than the norm. Coercive diplomacy has worked on a few occasions, such as in 2003, when the Libyan leader Muammar al-Qaddafi chose to stop developing weapons of mass destruction partly as a result of pressure and reassurances from the United States. More often than not, however, in recent decades the United States has failed at coercive diplomacy even though it has had overwhelming power and has made it clear that it will use force if necessary. A succession of relatively weak adversaries, including Panama (1989), Iraq (1990 and 2003), Serbia (1998), and Taliban-ruled Afghanistan (2001), did not respond to American attempts at pressure, leading Washington to fall back repeatedly on direct military action. Coercive diplomacy did convince the military junta that ruled Haiti to step down in 1994, but only once it was clear that U.S. warplanes were already in the air. And today, Iran is hardly alone in its defiance: despite issuing many threats and promises, the United States has been unable to persuade North Korea to relinquish its nuclear arsenal or even refrain from sharing its nuclear expertise with other countries (as it apparently did with Syria).

The threats and promises the United States has used with Iran are not inherently incompatible: Washington has said it will punish Tehran for proceeding with its nuclear program but is willing to cut a deal with it should the program be halted. Logically, these components could reinforce each other, as the former pushes and the latter pulls Iran toward an agreement. But the dreary history of coercive diplomacy shows that all too often, threats and promises undercut, rather than complement, each other.

Threats can prove particularly troublesome, since if they fail, they can drive the threatening party onto a path it may not actually want to follow. U.S. President John F. Kennedy learned this lesson during the 1962 Cuban missile crisis. Kennedy was mostly, but not completely, joking when he said, on learning that the Soviet Union had stationed warheads in Cuba, "Last month I said we weren't going to [allow it]. Last month I should have said we don't care." More important, ramping up threats can undermine the chances that promises will be taken seriously. Inflicting increasing pain and making explicit threats to continue to do so can also raise questions about whether the party inflicting the pain really wants a deal and raise the domestic costs to the suffering government of making concessions.

When the United States suggests that it is willing to bomb Iran if it does not negotiate away its weapons program, it implies that the Americans believe that the costs of military action are tolerable. Although this increases the credibility of the threat, it could also lead Iran to conclude that the United States sees the costs of bombing as low enough to make military action more attractive than any outcome short of a complete Iranian surrender. Moreover, because Iran's nuclear program is at least in part driven by the Islamic Republic's desire to be able to protect itself against attack, this U.S. threat is likely to heighten the perceived danger and so increase Iran's determination not to be swayed from its current course.

This does not mean that pressure is always counterproductive. According to U.S. intelligence agencies, the Iranians halted their development of nuclear weapons in 2003, presumably in response to the menace created by the U.S. invasion of Iraq. It appears that what a U.S. diplomat once said of North Korea also applies to Iran today: "The North Koreans do not respond to pressure. But without pressure they do not respond."

WHY THIS CASE IS EVEN HARDER

Even if pressure can work, and despite the fact that threats do not need to be completely credible in order to be effective, Washington faces daunting obstacles in trying to establish the credibility of its threat to strike Iran. What is most obvious, bombing would be very costly for the Americans (which is one of the reasons why it has not yet been done). As Tehran surely understands, Washington knows that the likely results include at least a small war in the region, deepening hostility to the United States around the world, increased domestic support for the Iranian regime, legitimation of the Iranian nuclear weapons program, and the need to strike again if Iran reconstitutes it. Given such high costs, Tehran might conclude that Washington's threat to bomb is just a bluff, and one it is willing to call.

Ironically, the success of economic sanctions could further diminish the credibility of the U.S. threat of a military strike. Iranian leaders might judge that their U.S. counterparts will continue to stick with sanctions in the hopes that the pain will ultimately yield a change in Iranian policy, or they might think that U.S. officials will hold off on the unpopular and unilateral military option to avoid disrupting the relatively popular and multilateral sanctions regime.

The credibility of Washington's threat to bomb is also affected by the perceptions and intentions of Iran's rulers. Iranian leaders might fall into the trap of basing their predictions about U.S. policy on their own expectations, which might differ from the Americans'. Those Iranians with relatively benign intentions toward the United States might expect that it would be fairly easy for the Americans to live with a nuclear-armed Iran, assume their U.S. counterparts will think similarly, and thus think a preventive U.S. military strike is unlikely. More aggressive Iranian leaders, on the other hand, might take the U.S. threat to bomb more seriously, since they themselves see Iran's acquisition of a bomb to be significant and assume their American counterparts will, too. These Iranian hawks might thus see U.S. preventive military action as plausible and expect it, moreover, to be aimed at broader goals, such as regime change, rather than simply setting back the Iranian nuclear program.

The history of U.S. policy toward Iran over the past decade will also complicate the credibility of American threats. On the one hand, the United States has imposed unilateral sanctions and skillfully mustered support from the Europeans for severe international sanctions. Many Western observers were surprised by this, and the Iranian leadership probably was, too. On the other hand, the United States has not bombed Iran despite continuing Iranian defiance of UN resolutions and U.S. policies. Iran also cannot have failed to notice that the United States did not attack North Korea as it developed its nuclear weapons, even after having repeatedly issued strong threats that it would do so. Moreover, Washington has been trying to coerce Iran into giving up its nuclear program for ages now, to little avail, making it hard to instill a sense of urgency in its current efforts.

Of course, threatening to bomb Iran's nuclear facilities is not the only form of pressure the United States can exert. Washington can maintain the current punishing sanctions regime indefinitely or even strengthen it. It could conduct additional covert actions, especially cyberattacks, to slow down the Iranian nuclear program.

Because these actions are less costly to pursue than a military strike, threatening them might be more credible. But it can be more difficult to make such threats effective. The Iranians understand that they will pay a price for moving forward on the nuclear front. To change their minds, therefore, outsiders will have to threaten or inflict even greater pain than the Iranians are expecting.

HOW TO MAKE CREDIBLE THREATS

There are various ways the United States can make its threats more credible. The first is to voice them publicly and unambiguously. Obama has already gone quite far in his public statements, so the low-hanging fruit in this area has been picked. If the confrontation continues, however, a concerted campaign to inform the American public about the impending risk of war would resonate strongly, especially if capped by a congressional resolution authorizing the possible use of force against Iran. If those steps failed to sway the Iranians, the United States could issue an ultimatum, sending a clear signal to all parties that time was running out for a peaceful solution to the crisis, although doing so would be highly controversial at home and abroad and would mean giving up the military advantages of surprise.

U.S. policymakers could also stop publicly expressing their reluctance to use force and instead emphasize that they think an attack on Iran would benefit the United States. They could claim to expect that a U.S. strike would deal a dramatic blow to Iran's nuclear effort, serve as a powerful warning to other potential proliferators, strengthen the United States' global reputation for resolve, and possibly even trigger an Iranian revolution.

Private threats at this point would probably add little, but threats delivered confidentially by third parties close to Tehran, such as China and Russia, might have more credibility, and these states might carry the message if they were convinced that the only alternative was U.S. military action. Conversely, Israeli statements expressing skepticism that the United States will ever bomb Iran have undercut Washington's position. If Israeli leaders were to stop such talk and start claiming that they are now confident that the United States is willing to strike if necessary (albeit not on the timetable that Israel would prefer), such a shift would be duly noted in Tehran.

The United States could also increase the credibility of its threats by specifying the Iranian actions that would trigger an attack. The fact that Obama has resisted calls to announce such "redlines" does not mean that he does not have them. It seems likely that the decision for a strike would be made if Iran got close enough to producing a nuclear weapon that it could do so quickly and stealthily, or began producing highly enriched uranium, or expelled the International Atomic Energy Agency's inspectors. Still, even if announcing specific redlines such as these would enhance U.S. credibility, it would have downsides as well. Specifying what would be prohibited would mark out what would be permitted, and Iran could take that as an invitation to move right up to the redlines.

Washington could lend its threats credibility through actions even more than through words. It could bolster its military capabilities in a way that demonstrated its seriousness, including making expensive preparations to deal with retaliation by Iran after an American attack. It could even begin military maneuvers that have some risk of provoking Iran and leading to escalation, thus showing that Washington is not frightened by the prospect of a fight developing accidentally.

U.S. threats could also be made more credible if Washington developed plans for a strike against Iranian nuclear facilities and then deliberately allowed Iranian intelligence services to learn the details. In this scenario, the Iranians would have to believe they discovered something the Americans had sought to hide from them, lest they conclude it was simply a ruse designed to impress them. This kind of maneuver is tricky: although sound in principle, in practice it has generally proved too clever by half. During the 1961 Berlin crisis, for example, the Kennedy administration provided West Germany with its plans for a military response to the standoff, knowing the West German government had been penetrated by Soviet intelligence. And in 1969, the Nixon administration staged an ostensibly secret nuclear-alert exercise designed to convey the strength of the U.S. commitment to South Vietnam. In both cases, however, the Soviets hardly noticed.

One might assume that the United States could increase the credibility of its threats in Iranian eyes by building up its defenses, seemingly in preparation for a possible conflict. But bulking up U.S. capabilities against Iranian missiles in the eastern Mediterranean and the Persian Gulf might also send the opposite signal—that the United States is preparing not to attack but rather to live with (and deter) a nuclear-armed Iran. Canceling the deployment of systems designed to defend against Iranian missiles, in fact, would be a strong and dramatic signal that the United States has no intention of allowing a nuclear Iran and is willing to strike preventively to head off such a prospect.

WHY IT'S HARD TO MAKE CREDIBLE PROMISES

In general, making promises credible is even harder than making threats credible, and that is especially true in this case because of the history of mutual mistrust and the conflicting historical narratives that each side tells itself. U.S. promises to Iran are complicated by other factors as well. There are multiple audiences listening in on anything Washington says to Tehran: domestic constituencies, Arab states, North Korea, other states that might seek nuclear weapons, and, of course, Israel. The fear of an Israeli attack may provide a useful source of extra pressure, but Iranian perceptions of U.S.-Israeli collusion can make U.S. signaling to Iran more difficult. American promises must be seen to cover Israeli actions as well, and some promises designed to reassure Israel of U.S. protection might conflict with conciliatory messages Washington wishes to send to Tehran.

U.S. policymakers also have limited knowledge of Iranian perceptions and domestic politics. It is generally agreed that Iran's nuclear policy rests in the hands of the country's supreme leader, Ayatollah Ali Khamenei. But it is hard to know just what his goals are, how he perceives U.S. messages, and even which messages are accurately conveyed to him. If history is any lesson, the likelihood is that he interprets much American behavior, including promises, in ways that Americans would find utterly bizarre.

Just what various Iranian actors would perceive as a reward, moreover, might be hard to determine. Some figures in or close to the regime, for example, have built fortunes and political power bases around adapting to sanctions, so removing or loosening sanctions might actually harm rather than help them. Even the most valuable prize the West could offer—the normalization of relations and the integration of the Islamic Republic into the world community—could conflict with the worldview of dominant actors in Iran, undercut their power, and be seen by them, quite possibly accurately, as a step toward eventual regime change.

All these gaps in knowledge and trust stand in the way of the United States' ability to make credible promises of any kind to Iran, whether minor assurances intended to serve as confidence-building measures or the more substantial promises that could lead to a durable diplomatic settlement. In the most likely deal, Iran would agree to stop designing warheads and to refrain from enriching uranium above the 20 percent level. It would retain only limited stockpiles of uranium enriched to 5–20 percent, accept limits on the capacities of its enrichment facilities, allow robust inspections of its nuclear facilities, and agree to refrain from building facilities that the United States could not destroy. (Such a deal would permit the heavily fortified underground Fordow enrichment plant to remain open, since it is vulnerable to a U.S. strike—something that would displease the Israelis, whose own capabilities are insufficient to overcome Fordow's defenses.)

In return, the United States would accept a limited Iranian enrichment program, promise not to try to overthrow the regime (and maybe not to undermine it), and suspend sanctions that were imposed specifically in response to the nuclear program. The United States might also restore normal diplomatic relations with Iran—although taking that step, along with lifting other sanctions, might require a larger grand bargain involving Iran's ending its support for Hamas and Hezbollah.

To convince Iran that such a deal is possible, the United States would have to surmount four barriers. It would need to gain some measure of Israeli acquiescence, both to satisfy influential pro-Israel constituencies in the United States and to convince Iran that the deal would not be undercut by Israeli sabotage, assassinations, or attacks. Accepting a civilian nuclear program in Iran would necessitate repealing or carving out some sort of exception to various UN Security Council resolutions, because the original sanctions were applied in response to the establishment of the nuclear program itself, not to the subsequent progress Iran has apparently made.

Washington would need to convince Tehran that negotiations were not designed to weaken it and that a settlement would end American efforts at regime change. Security assurances would have to be part of any deal, and they would be hard to craft. The fact that the United States helped overthrow Qaddafi in 2011 despite his earlier agreement to abandon his weapons of mass destruction program would surely be on Iranian minds.

Finally, the United States would have to find some way of offering Iran intangible goods it truly craves: respect and treatment as an equal. Not only can the process of hard bargaining get in the way of respectful treatment, but so can even the imagery used to think about such bargaining—such as talk of "carrots and sticks," which implies that Iran is an animal that the West is trying to manipulate. On the other hand, showing respect to Iran would not cost the United States a great deal.

GETTING TO THE TABLE

Although the United States and its European allies are talking with Iran now, these conversations seem to involve little more than recitations of unyielding opening positions. Distrust is often highest at the beginning of a negotiation process, since both sides fear that any preliminary concessions will not only be pocketed but also be taken as a sign of weakness that will embolden the other side to hold out for more.

There are standard, if imperfect, ways to deal with this problem, such as by using disavowable third parties who can float enticing ideas without exposing actual negotiating positions. Ambiguous "feelers" are also useful, since they require the other side to respond to a message before its true meaning is revealed and so limit the first state's exposure. But the distrust between the United States and Iran runs so deep that the normal playbook is unlikely to work here. Getting through to the supreme leader and convincing him that serious negotiations are in his interest will be difficult. Appealing to him personally and directly, in both public and private, might be effective, as might sending a high-level emissary (although such steps should be reserved until close to the last possible minute, to avoid undue humiliation should they fail).

A dramatic (if unlikely) approach would be for the United States to unilaterally suspend some of its sanctions against Iran, halt all its military preparations related to Iran, or declare that the option of using force is no longer on the table. A more plausible scenario would be for U.S. leaders to try to communicate that they are ready for an agreement by letting the Iranian regime know that they are studying how to suspend sanctions in stages and developing various forms of security guarantees.

The normal negotiating procedure would be to start with small confidence-building measures and put off dealing with the central and most difficult issues for while, until some progress and mutual trust have been achieved. It is probably too late for that, however, especially since many of the standard smaller steps have been removed from consideration by the recent application of even tougher international sanctions on Iran. Until recently, for example, a freeze-for-freeze approach to confidence building might have been possible: a U.S. offer to take no further aggressive steps in exchange for a comparable Iranian move. But at this point, given the pain the sanctions are currently inflicting, modifying them or suspending them would probably be required, which would be a much bigger concession on the part of the United States and Europe.

It will probably be necessary for Washington to sketch the broad contours of a possible final agreement before talks begin. Entering serious negotiations would carry high political costs for the White House and spark a major political struggle in Tehran—risks the leaders on each side would take only if there seemed to be good prospects of an acceptable solution. And any agreement, of course, would have to be carried out incrementally in order for each side to guard against the other's reneging.

Still, the United States may need to put more of its cards on the table at the start. It will have to convince Khamenei that successful negotiations would greatly reduce the threat to his country posed by the United States and that Washington would be willing to accept an appropriately safeguarded Iranian civilian nuclear program. There will be a strong temptation in Washington to reserve such inducements for the final stage of hard bargaining, but holding them back is likely to greatly decrease the chance that the negotiations will reach that stage at all.

The obstacles to successful negotiations may be so great that the best the United States can achieve is a form of containment that would maintain something like the status quo, with Iran remaining at some distance from a weapon. Such a situation might not be stable, however, and what Soviet Premier Nikita Khrushchev told Kennedy at the height of the Cuban missile crisis could also prove relevant to the U.S.-Iranian confrontation: "Mr. President, we and you ought not now to pull on the end of the rope in which you have tied the knot of war, because the more the two of us pull, the tighter the knot will be tied. And a moment may come when that knot will be tied so tight that even he who tied it will not have the strength to untie it. And then it will be necessary to cut that knot."

Looking carefully at the challenges of coercive diplomacy in this case is sobering. Using threats and promises to successfully manage the problems posed by Iran's nuclear program will be difficult at best, requiring extraordinary levels of calmness, boldness, creativity, and forbearance. But if Washington is determined to avoid both military action and deterrence, those are the qualities it will need to summon.

The Lost Logic of Deterrence

What the Strategy That Won the Cold War Can—and Can't—Do Now

Richard K. Betts

Deterrence isn't what it used to be. In the second half of the twentieth century, it was the backbone of U.S. national security. Its purpose, logic, and effectiveness were well understood. It was the essential military strategy behind containing the Soviet Union and a crucial ingredient in winning the Cold War without fighting World War III. But in recent decades, deterrence has gone astray, and U.S. defense policy is worse for the change.

Since the Cold War ended, the United States has clung to deterrence where it should not have, needlessly aggravating relations with Russia. More important, it has rejected deterrence where it should have embraced it, leading to one unnecessary and disastrous war with Iraq and the risk of another with Iran. And most important, with regard to China, Washington is torn about whether or not to rely on deterrence at all, even though such confusion could lead to a crisis and a dangerous miscalculation in Beijing.

Mistakes in applying deterrence have come from misunderstandings about the concept itself, faulty threat assessments, forgetfulness

RICHARD K. BETTS is Director of the Saltzman Institute of War and Peace Studies at Columbia University and an Adjunct Senior Fellow at the Council on Foreign Relations. His most recent book is *American Force: Dangers, Delusions, and Dilemmas in National Security*.

about history, and shortsighted policymaking. Bringing these problems into focus can restore faith in deterrence where it has been lost, lower costs where the strategy has been misapplied, and reduce the danger of surprise in situations where the risk of conflict is unclear.

Deterrence is a strategy for combining two competing goals: countering an enemy and avoiding war. Academics have explored countless variations on that theme, but the basic concept is quite simple: an enemy will not strike if it knows the defender can defeat the attack or can inflict unacceptable damage in retaliation.

At best, applying deterrence when it is unneeded wastes resources. At worst, it may provoke conflict rather than hold it in check. And even when deterrence is appropriate, it might not work—for example, against an enemy who is suicidal or invulnerable to a counterattack. Thus, it is more useful against governments, which have a return address and want to survive, than against terrorists who cannot be found or who do not fear death. Deterrence is also a weak tool in the increasingly important realm of cyberspace, where it can be extremely difficult to be absolutely sure of an attacker's identity.

When the United States does choose to apply deterrence and is willing to fight, the deterrent warning must be loud and clear, so the target cannot misread it. Deterrence should be ambiguous only if it is a bluff. One of the biggest dangers, however, comes in the reverse situation, when Washington fails to declare deterrence in advance but then decides to fight when an unexpected attack comes. That kind of confusion caused the United States to suddenly enter both the Korean War and the Gulf War, despite official statements in both cases that had led the aggressors to believe it would not.

Deterrence is not a strategy for all seasons. It does not guarantee success. There are risks in relying on it and also in rejecting it when the alternatives are worse.

UNNECESSARY ROUGHNESS

To Moscow, it must seem that the Cold War is only half over, since the West's deterrence posture, although muted, lives on. During the Cold War, deterrence was vital because the Soviet threat seemed huge. Moscow's military capabilities included some 175 divisions aimed at Western Europe and close to 40,000 nuclear weapons. Soviet intentions were much debated, but they were officially assumed to be very hostile. The West's response was to deploy ample military counterpower via NATO and the U.S. Strategic Air Command. And for more than 40 years, deterrence held. Despite tense crises over Berlin and Cuba and proxy conflicts in the Third World, Moscow never dared unleash its forces directly against the West. Doves doubted that so much deterrence was necessary, but hawks were reassured that against a potent threat, deterrence did not fail.

Yet implicit deterrence persisted after the West's victory because of demands from members of the old Warsaw Pact that joined NATO, the retrograde politics of the post-Soviet Russian state, and sheer force of habit. The 2012 Republican U.S. presidential candidate Mitt Romney was only channeling a common view when he said that Russia remained the United States' "number one geopolitical foe."

Although most of the remaining U.S. military infrastructure committed to NATO provides logistical support for missions "out of area," and despite the tightening of the U.S. defense budget, two U.S. brigade combat teams are still stationed in Europe. These might seem only symbolic, but together with NATO's expansion, they appear aimed at Moscow. The United States and Russia also continue to negotiate with each other over their nuclear arsenals. But there is no reason for formal arms control between countries unless they fear each other's forces, feel the need to limit what they could do to each other in the event of war, and want to institutionalize mutual deterrence.

These continuities with the Cold War would make sense only between intense adversaries. Washington and Moscow remain in an adversarial relationship, but not an intense one. If the Cold War is really over, and the West really won, then continuing implicit deterrence does less to protect against a negligible threat from

Russia than to feed suspicions that aggravate political friction. In contrast to during the Cold War, it is now hard to make the case that Russia is more a threat to NATO than the reverse. First, the East-West balance of military capabilities, which at the height of the Cold War was favorable to the Warsaw Pact or at best even, has not only shifted to NATO's advantage; it has become utterly lopsided. Russia is now a lonely fraction of what the old Warsaw Pact was. It not only lost its old eastern European allies; those allies are now arrayed on the other side, as members of NATO. By every significant measure of power—military spending, men under arms, population, economic strength, control of territory—NATO enjoys massive advantages over Russia. The only capability that keeps Russia militarily potent is its nuclear arsenal. There is no plausible way, however, that Moscow's nuclear weapons could be used for aggression, except as a backstop for a conventional offensive—for which NATO's capabilities are now far greater.

Russia's intentions constitute no more of a threat than its capabilities. Although Moscow's ruling elites push distasteful policies, there is no plausible way they could think a military attack on the West would serve their interests. During the twentieth century, there were intense territorial conflicts between the two sides and a titanic struggle between them over whose ideology would dominate the world. Vladimir Putin's Russia is authoritarian, but unlike the Soviet Union, it is not the vanguard of a globe-spanning revolutionary ideal.

The imbalance of capabilities between NATO and Russia does not mean that Moscow's interests are of no concern, or that the United States can rub the Russians' noses in their military inferiority with impunity. Russia is still a major power whose future policies and alignment matter. Indeed, if Russia were to align with a rising China, the strategic implications for the United States would not be trivial. Too many Americans blithely assume that continued Chinese-Russian antagonism is inevitable; in fact, Japan, NATO, and the United States are providing China and Russia with incentives to put aside their differences and make common cause against pressure from the West.

Even absent a Chinese-Russian partnership, confronting Russia poses unnecessary risks. The only unresolved territorial issues in the region are more important to Moscow than to the West, as the 2008 miniwar between Georgia and Russia demonstrated. If NATO were to expand deterrence even further by admitting Georgia as a member—a move the Obama administration supports in principle, as did the George W. Bush administration—it would be a direct challenge to Moscow's protection of secessionist regions in the country. It would constitute a frank statement that Russia can have no sphere of interest at all, one of the usual prerogatives of a major power. NATO would thus finish the job of turning deterrence into forthright domination—precisely what China and the Soviet Union used to falsely claim was the real intention of the West's deterrent posture. In the worst case, admitting Georgia into NATO could be the last straw for Russia, precipitating a crisis.

The cost of either of those outcomes would be higher than the price of a more decisive Western military stand-down and an end to talk of expanding NATO further. Stable peace with an uncongenial regime in Moscow should be a higher priority than unconditional backing for Russia's closest neighbors. Ultimately, however, as long as NATO is an alliance that excludes Russia, rather than a genuine collective security organization, which would have to include Russia, Moscow will inevitably interpret its very existence as a threat. The consolidation of peace in Europe will not be complete as long as practically every European country belongs to NATO except Russia. The idea of Russian membership is fanciful so far; there is no movement for it in the West, nor any indication that Moscow would join even if invited. But Russian claims that NATO is a threat would be easier to discredit if its members appeared willing to consider inviting Russia to join, if it gets back on the path to democracy.

LESSONS UNLEARNED

Too much deterrence of Russia is a mistake, but not as serious as the opposite mistake: rejecting deterrence where it is badly needed. That mistake is harming U.S. efforts to cope with nuclear proliferation and, most particularly, Iran. Instead of planning to deter would-be proliferators, U.S. policymakers have developed a preference for preventive war. They now seem to fear that deterrence is too weak to deal with radical regimes, forgetting that the precise purpose of deterrence is to counter dangerous enemies, not cautious ones. This preference is especially troubling because it continues even after two painful experiences with Iraq that vividly highlighted why deterrence is the better choice.

Deterrence played no role in the run-up to the first major conflict after the Cold War, the 1990-91 Gulf War. The assault by Saddam Hussein on Kuwait was widely misread as showing that he was undeterrable. It showed no such thing, however, because the United States had not tried to deter him. Had Saddam known that invading Kuwait would spur Washington to launch a decisive war against him, he surely would have refrained. But the administration of George H. W. Bush never made such a threat, and the dictator was left free to miscalculate.

Bush had been unprepared to make a deterrent threat because an Iraqi invasion of Kuwait was a totally unexpected contingency. This situation was exactly the same as the one that had produced an unexpected and avoidable war 40 years earlier. In 1949, U.S. Army General Douglas MacArthur publicly stated that South Korea did not fall within the U.S. defense perimeter in Asia; the following year, U.S. Secretary of State Dean Acheson made comments to the same effect. These statements reflected the fact that the United States was planning for a third world war, in which Korea would be a low priority—which is why President Harry Truman was completely surprised when the North attacked the South in the absence of a broader war.

In 2003, George W. Bush did not have the excuse of surprise. He deliberately chose not to rely on deterring Iraq, deciding instead to start a war immediately in order to prevent Iraq from possibly using weapons of mass destruction sometime in the future. The result was a disaster.

It is impossible to know whether the alternative of relying on deterrence to keep Saddam in check would have produced a bigger disaster, as the war's instigators asserted. There is no evidence, however, that Saddam could not have been deterred indefinitely. He had indulged in wanton aggression against Iran in 1980 and Kuwait a decade later, but these were cases in which he had reason to believe that he faced no daunting counterpower. He was a reckless bully, but not suicidal. He never attacked in the face of a U.S. threat to respond, nor did he use his chemical or biological weapons even in defense against the U.S. assault in 1991, when Washington exercised deterrence by warning of devastating retaliation in the face of such an attack.

American fears of Saddam—and now of Iran's leaders—seem exaggerated in light of the United States' experience during the Cold War. Presidents considered but rejected preventive war against Mao and Stalin, who seemed even more fanatical and aggressive in their time than today's foes. Mao issued chilling statements unmatched by anything yet heard from leaders in Tehran—for example, that the prospect of nuclear war "is not a bad thing" because defeating capitalism would be worth losing up to two-thirds of the world's population.

Considering the positive results of Cold War containment and the awful miscarriage of a preventive strategy against Iraq, one might have expected U.S. policymakers to find deterrence attractive as a fallback strategy to deal with Iran if the Islamic Republic could not be dissuaded from developing nuclear weapons. After all, that is precisely how Washington has dealt with a nuclear-armed North Korea. But U.S. and Israeli leaders have convinced themselves that Iran might one day use nuclear weapons for aggression—irrationally and without provocation. There is no evidence, however, that the Iranian leadership has any interest in national suicide, the likely consequence of an Iranian nuclear first strike. Iran has supported terrorism, justifying it as a response to American and Israeli covert warfare. But however aggressive its motives, the revolutionary regime in Tehran has never launched a regular war against its enemies.

Nevertheless, rather than planning to deter a prospective Iranian nuclear arsenal, the United States and Israel have preferred preventive war. Although many still hope to turn Iran away from nuclear weapons through sanctions and diplomacy, the debate within and between the United States and Israel over what to do if Iran moves to produce a bomb is about not whether to attack but when. U.S. President Barack Obama has firmly declared that he has not a "policy of containment" but rather "a policy to prevent Iran from obtaining a nuclear weapon," and other administration officials have repeatedly emphasized this point. As promises in foreign policy go, this one is chiseled in stone. Backing down from it when the time comes would be the right thing to do but would represent an embarrassing retreat.

The logic behind rejecting deterrence is that Tehran might decide to use nuclear weapons despite facing devastating retaliation. The risk can never be reduced to zero, but there is no reason to believe that Iran poses more danger than other nasty regimes that have already developed nuclear weapons. The most telling example is North Korea. Although the American public has not paid nearly as much attention to North Korea, Pyongyang's record of fanatical belligerence and terrorist behavior over the years has been far worse than Tehran's.

Refusing to accept an iota of risk from Iran ignores the massive risks of the alternative of initiating war. Leaving aside the danger of being blind-sided by unanticipated forms of Iranian reprisal—for example, the use of biological weapons—the obvious risks include Iranian retaliation by overt or covert military means against U.S. assets. The results of the initially successful assault on Iraq in 2003 are a reminder that wars the United States starts do not necessarily end when and how it wants them to. Indeed, the records of the United States and Israel suggest that both countries tend to underestimate the prospective costs of the wars they enter. Washington paid fewer costs than expected during the Gulf War but faced a far higher bill than anticipated in Korea, Vietnam, Kosovo, Afghanistan, and the second war against Iraq. Israel suffered less in the 1967 Six-Day War than expected but was badly surprised by the costs of the 1973 Yom Kippur War, the 1982 Lebanon war, and the 2006 war against Hezbollah.

Launching a war against Iran would also have negative spillover effects. First and foremost, short of an accompanying ground invasion and occupation, an air attack could not guarantee an end to Iran's pursuit of nuclear weapons; it could guarantee only a delay and would almost certainly drive the Iranians to commit more fervently to building a bomb. If Iran's capabilities were only temporarily degraded but its intentions were inflamed, the threat might become worse. Striking first would also fracture the international coalition that now stands behind sanctions against Iran, undercut opposition to the regime inside the country, and be seen throughout the world as another case of arrogant American aggression against Muslims.

Those costs might seem justifiable if launching a war against Iran dissuaded other countries from attempting to get their own nuclear deterrents. But it might just as well energize such efforts. George W. Bush's war to prevent Iraq from getting nuclear weapons did not dissuade North Korea, which went on to test its own weapons a few years later, nor did it turn Iran away. It may have induced Libyan leader Muammar al-Qaddafi to surrender his nuclear program, but a few years later, his reward from Washington turned out to be overthrow and death—hardly an encouraging lesson for U.S. adversaries about the wisdom of renouncing nuclear weapons.

One reason U.S. leaders might be reluctant to apply deterrence these days is that the strategy's most potent form—the threat to annihilate an enemy's economy and population in retaliation—is no longer deemed legitimate. In 1945, hardly any Americans objected to the incineration of hundreds of thousands of Japanese civilians, and throughout the Cold War, few objected to the principle of killing on an even greater scale in retaliation for a Soviet attack. But times have changed: today, post-Cold War norms and

Pentagon lawyers have put the idea of deliberately targeting civilians thoroughly out of bounds. It would be difficult for the U.S. government to declare that if one Iranian nuclear weapon was detonated somewhere, it would kill millions of Iranians in return.

But that inhibition should hardly be a reason to prefer starting a war, nor does it cripple deterrence. An acceptable variant would be to threaten not to annihilate Iran's population but to annihilate its regime—the leaders, security agencies, and assets of the Iranian government—if it used nuclear weapons. Although in practice, even a discriminating counterattack of that kind would result in plenty of collateral damage, U.S. planners could credibly make the threat and could reinforce it by pledging to invade Iran as well—a step that would be far more reasonable to take after an Iranian nuclear strike than it was against Iraq in 2003. And even if legal concerns constrained the United States from massively retaliating against Iranian civilians, Israeli leaders would surely be willing to do so if Iran attacked Israel with nuclear weapons, since Israel's national existence would be at stake. Those mutually reinforcing threats—that the fruits of the Iranian Revolution and even Iranian society itself would cease to exist—would be an overwhelming restraint on Tehran.

A nuclear-armed Iran is an alarming prospect. But there is no sure solution to some dangers, and this challenge presents a strategic choice between different risks. There is simply no real evidence that war with Iran would yield any more safety than handling the problem with good old deterrence.

MIXED SIGNALS

The most dangerous long-term risk posed by Washington's confusion over deterrence lies in the avoidance of a choice one way or the other about the strategy when it comes to China. Washington needs to determine whether to treat Beijing as a threat to be contained or a power to be accommodated. U.S. policymakers have long tried to have it both ways. Such incoherence is politically natural but harmless only so long as no catalyst exposes the contradiction. It will thus prove unsustainable unless China decides to act indefinitely with more humility than any other rising power in history has and unless it feels less sense of entitlement than the United States does itself.

One influential view has held that deterrence is a nonissue for U.S.-Chinese relations because the two states' economic interdependence precludes military conflict. In this view, confrontation is nonsensical, so preparing for it only risks turning it into a self-fulfilling prophecy. The opposing view, that China's rising power is a threat that must be countered militarily, has been gaining but has not been turned into explicit policy. Meanwhile, the Obama administration's declared "pivot," or "rebalancing," of American military power toward Asia has not been accompanied by consistent signals about where, when, why, or how U.S. armed forces would be sent into combat against China, nor is there a clear operational rationale for basing a contingent of U.S. marines in Australia, the most concrete symbol of the pivot. The problem is not that deterrence has been inappropriately rejected or embraced but that it is muddled.

Adding to this lack of clarity, Washington continues to ignore the question of when and how Beijing's long patience about resolving Taiwan's status could end. China has always made clear that the question of reunification is a matter of when, not whether. For years, Washington has kicked the can down the road by warning Taipei not to declare independence, a provocation that Beijing has said would trigger military action. But when asked in 2001 what the United States would do to defend Taiwan, Bush declared, "Whatever it takes." In effect, U.S. policy has evolved into a promise to defend Taiwan as long as it is a rebellious province of China, but not if it is a separate country. This stance strikes some experts as a clever solution—but it defies most Americans' common sense, sends an ambiguous signal to Beijing, and thus undermines Washington's readiness for a crisis.

Meanwhile, conflicts brew, such as the recent revival of tensions over disputed islands in the South China Sea. Preoccupied with other strategic challenges, Washington is drifting toward unanticipated confrontation, without a clear decision about the circumstances in which it would be willing to go to war with China. This distraction and hesitancy prevent the sending of clear warnings to Beijing of U.S. "redlines," increasing the risks of an inadvertent crisis, miscalculation, and escalation.

Chinese and Philippine naval maneuvers near disputed islands in mid-2012 were a wake-up call, and subsequent jockeying by China and Japan over the even more dangerous disagreement over who owns the Diaoyu/Senkaku Islands put Washington's confusion into stark relief. The initial U.S. response to the latter dispute was a disturbing contradiction: "We don't take a position on the islands, but we do assert that they are covered under the treaty," a State Department spokesperson declared, referring to the mutual security agreement between Japan and the United States. Secretary of Defense Leon Panetta then said that the United States would not take sides in regional disputes over territory and also claimed that although U.S. strategic rebalancing toward Asia is more than mere rhetoric, it is not a threat to China.

All of this is ambivalent deterrence: rhetorical bobbing and weaving rather than strategic planning. It is a dangerous practice, projecting provocation and weakness at the same time. Washington signals Beijing not to occupy the various islands but does not threaten to block it from doing so, even while assuring Tokyo that the United States is treaty-bound to defend the islands. Subsequent clarifications or secret statements to either capital might mitigate the contradiction, but the public posture subverts U.S. credibility. It invites Chinese leaders to see the United States as a paper tiger that may fold in an escalating crisis. Yet in such a crisis, under the pressure of events for which it has not prepared, Washington might surprise its opponent by choosing war, for the same reasons it did so after the invasion of South Korea in 1950 and Kuwait in 1990.

There are two logical long-term alternatives to this risky confusion. One is to make a clear commitment to contain China, meaning that Washington would block Beijing from expanding its territory through either military action or political coercion. This sounds precipitate, because China sees containment as an aggressive threat. So Washington would have to express this commitment carefully, emphasizing the defensive aim of securing the status quo, not challenging China's rights. The benefit of this alternative would be to make deterrence harder to mistake and thus more effective, allowing for brighter redlines, which would reduce the odds of an unanticipated game of chicken producing a war neither side wants. But the costs would be very high: a new Cold War and the disruption of advantageous cooperation on many issues. The United States would also have to decide once and for all whether it is willing to go to war with China over Taiwan. At present, there is no serious discussion about this, let alone consensus, among either U.S. voters or the foreign policy elite in Washington.

If a "red light" strategy of containment is unnecessary or too costly, the second, opposite alternative is accommodation—in effect, a green light. Accommodation would make sense if Beijing's ambitions were limited and likely to stay limited, if its growing power was not in danger of being derailed, and if the United States preferred disregarding the interests of its allies to growing conflict with an emerging superpower—all big ifs. In accommodating Beijing, Washington would recognize that as China becomes a superpower, it will naturally feel entitled to the prerogatives of a superpower—most obviously, disproportionate influence in its home region. And Washington would have to accept that disputes over minor issues will be settled on China's terms rather than those of its weak neighbors. The big obstacle to this alternative would be the conflict over Taiwan, a far more consequential dispute than those over the uninhabited rocks whose status provoked tensions last year. And just as there is no consensus for containment, Americans loathe anything that reeks of appeasement.

Given the unattractiveness of either alternative, it is no surprise that Washington has finessed the question. Incoherent compromise is a common and sometimes sensible diplomatic strategy. In

Asia, however, it means underestimating the risks of drift and indecision if Chinese power grows and Chinese restraint diminishes. U.S. policy now amounts to a yellow light, a warning to slow down, short of a firm requirement to stop. Yellow lights, however, tempt some drivers to speed up.

There is no pain-free solution to the problem posed by China's ascent, unless Taiwan surrenders peacefully. Kicking the can down the road might work for a long time, but only as long as Chinese forbearance lasts. If a crisis erupts, ambivalent deterrence may cause conflict rather than prevent it. It might prove too weak to make Beijing swerve first, but strong enough to keep Washington from swerving also, thus causing a collision. The only solution is a clear strategic decision about whether the United States will accept China's full claims as a superpower when it becomes one or draw clear redlines before a crisis comes.

Deterrence is not disastrous when applied mildly, although unnecessarily, to Russia, but it does have negative effects. Deterrence is not a sure thing against Iran, but it beats starting a war, especially a war that could make the ultimate threat worse. And in the face of the serious long-term policy dilemma posed by China, opting for or against deterrence is an extraordinarily hard choice, but avoiding the choice makes the dilemma ever more dangerous. Reducing future risks requires paying some immediate costs.

Getting deterrence back into focus will help fix these strategic problems. In the Cold War, the strategy was so ingrained and pervasive an element of U.S. strategy that "deterrence" became a buzzword used to justify everything in defense policy. In recent years, however, it has almost vanished from the vocabulary of strategic debate. U.S. policymakers need to relearn the basics of deterrence and rediscover its promise as a strategy in the right circumstances, while recognizing its drawbacks in others. The alternative of continued confusion will not matter, until it does—for example, whenever Beijing decides that the day has come for the changes it has always said were only a matter of time.

The Cuban Missile Crisis at 50

Lessons for U.S. Foreign Policy Today

Graham Allison

Fifty years ago, the Cuban missile crisis brought the world to the brink of nuclear disaster. During the standoff, U.S. President John F. Kennedy thought the chance of escalation to war was "between 1 in 3 and even," and what we have learned in later decades has done nothing to lengthen those odds. We now know, for example, that in addition to nuclear-armed ballistic missiles, the Soviet Union had deployed 100 tactical nuclear weapons to Cuba, and the local Soviet commander there could have launched these weapons without additional codes or commands from Moscow. The U.S. air strike and invasion that were scheduled for the third week of the confrontation would likely have triggered a nuclear response against American ships and troops, and perhaps even Miami. The resulting war might have led to the deaths of 100 million Americans and over 100 million Russians.

The main story line of the crisis is familiar. In October 1962, a U.S. spy plane caught the Soviet Union attempting to sneak nuclear-tipped missiles into Cuba, 90 miles off the United States' coast. Kennedy determined at the outset that this could not stand.

GRAHAM ALLISON is Professor of Government and Director of the Belfer Center for Science and International Affairs at Harvard University's Kennedy School of Government.

After a week of secret deliberations with his most trusted advisers, he announced the discovery to the world and imposed a naval blockade on further shipments of armaments to Cuba. The blockade prevented additional materiel from coming in but did nothing to stop the Soviets from operationalizing the missiles already there. And a tense second week followed during which Kennedy and Soviet Premier Nikita Khrushchev stood "eyeball to eyeball," neither side backing down.

Saturday, October 27, was the day of decision. Thanks to secret tapes Kennedy made of the deliberations, we can be flies on the wall, listening to the members of the president's ad hoc Executive Committee of the National Security Council, or ExComm, debate choices they knew could lead to nuclear Armageddon. At the last minute, the crisis was resolved without war, as Khrushchev accepted a final U.S. offer pledging not to invade Cuba in exchange for the withdrawal of the Soviet missiles.

Every president since Kennedy has tried to learn from what happened in that confrontation. Ironically, half a century later, with the Soviet Union itself only a distant memory, the lessons of the crisis for current policy have never been greater. Today, it can help U.S. policymakers understand what to do—and what not to do—about Iran, North Korea, China, and presidential decision-making in general.

WHAT WOULD KENNEDY DO?

The current confrontation between the United States and Iran is like a Cuban missile crisis in slow motion. Events are moving, seemingly inexorably, toward a showdown in which the U.S. president will be forced to choose between ordering a military attack and acquiescing to a nuclear-armed Iran.

Those were, in essence, the two options Kennedy's advisers gave him on the final Saturday: attack or accept Soviet nuclear missiles in Cuba. But Kennedy rejected both. Instead of choosing between them, he crafted an imaginative alternative with three components: a public deal in which the United States pledged not to invade

Cuba if the Soviet Union withdrew its missiles, a private ultimatum threatening to attack Cuba within 24 hours unless Khrushchev accepted that offer, and a secret sweetener that promised the withdrawal of U.S. missiles from Turkey within six months after the crisis was resolved. The sweetener was kept so secret that even most members of the ExComm deliberating with Kennedy on the final evening were in the dark, unaware that during the dinner break, the president had sent his brother Bobby to deliver this message to the Soviet ambassador.

Looking at the choice between acquiescence and air strikes today, both are unattractive. An Iranian bomb could trigger a cascade of proliferation, making more likely a devastating conflict in one of the world's most economically and strategically critical regions. A preventive air strike could delay Iran's nuclear progress at identified sites but could not erase the knowledge and skills ingrained in many Iranian heads. The truth is that any outcome that stops short of Iran having a nuclear bomb will still leave it with the ability to acquire one down the road, since Iran has already crossed the most significant "redline" of proliferation: mastering the art of enriching uranium and building a bomb covertly. The best hope for a Kennedyesque third option today is a combination of agreed-on constraints on Iran's nuclear activities that would lengthen the fuse on the development of a bomb, transparency measures that would maximize the likelihood of discovering any cheating, unambiguous (perhaps secretly communicated) threats of a regime-changing attack should the agreement be violated, and a pledge not to attack otherwise. Such a combination would keep Iran as far away from a bomb as possible for as long as possible.

The Israeli factor makes the Iranian nuclear situation an even more complex challenge for American policymakers than the Cuban missile crisis was. In 1962, only two players were allowed at the main table. Cuban Prime Minister Fidel Castro sought to become the third, and had he succeeded, the crisis would have become significantly more dangerous. (When Khrushchev announced the withdrawal of the missiles, for example, Castro sent him a blistering message urging him to fire those already in Cuba.) But precisely because the White House recognized that the Cubans could become a wild card, it cut them out of the game. Kennedy informed the Kremlin that it would be held accountable for any attack against the United States emanating from Cuba, however it started. His first public announcement said, "It shall be the policy of this Nation to regard any nuclear missile launched from Cuba against any nation in the Western Hemisphere as an attack by the Soviet Union on the United States, requiring a full retaliatory response upon the Soviet Union."

Today, the threat of an Israeli air strike strengthens U.S. President Barack Obama's hand in squeezing Iran to persuade it to make concessions. But the possibility that Israel might actually carry out a unilateral air strike without U.S. approval must make Washington nervous, since it makes the crisis much harder to manage. Should the domestic situation in Israel reduce the likelihood of an independent Israeli attack, U.S. policymakers will not be unhappy.

CARROTS GO BETTER WITH STICKS

Presented with intelligence showing Soviet missiles in Cuba, Kennedy confronted the Soviet Union publicly and demanded their withdrawal, recognizing that a confrontation risked war. Responding to North Korea's provocations over the years, in contrast, U.S. presidents have spoken loudly but carried a small stick. This is one reason the Cuban crisis was not repeated whereas the North Korean ones have been, repeatedly.

In confronting Khrushchev, Kennedy ordered actions that he knew would increase the risk not only of conventional war but also of nuclear war. He raised the U.S. nuclear alert status to DEFCON 2, aware that this would loosen control over the country's nuclear weapons and increase the likelihood that actions by other individuals could trigger a cascade beyond his control. For example, NATO aircraft with Turkish pilots loaded active nuclear bombs and advanced to an alert status in which individual pilots could have chosen to take off, fly to Moscow, and drop a bomb. Kennedy thought it necessary to increase the risks of war in the short run in order to decrease them over the longer term. He was thinking not only about Cuba but also about the next confrontation, which would most likely come over West Berlin, a free enclave inside the East German puppet state. Success in Cuba would embolden Khrushchev to resolve the Berlin situation on his own terms, forcing Kennedy to choose between accepting Soviet domination of the city and using nuclear weapons to try to save it.

During almost two dozen face-offs with North Korea over the past three decades, meanwhile, U.S. and South Korean policymakers have shied away from such risks, demonstrating that they are deterred by North Korea's threat to destroy Seoul in a second Korean war. North Korean leaders have taken advantage of this fear to develop an effective strategy for blackmail. It begins with an extreme provocation, blatantly crossing a redline that the United States has set out, along with a threat that any response will lead to a "sea of fire." After tensions have risen, a third party, usually China, steps in to propose that "all sides" step back and cool down. Soon thereafter, side payments to North Korea are made by South Korea or Japan or the United States, leading to a resumption of talks. After months of negotiations, Pyongyang agrees to accept still more payments in return for promises to abandon its nuclear program. Some months after that, North Korea violates the agreement, Washington and Seoul express shock, and they vow never to be duped again. And then, after a decent interval, the cycle starts once more.

If the worst consequence of this charade were simply the frustration of being bested by one of the poorest, most isolated states on earth, then the repeated Korean crises would be a sideshow. But for decades, U.S. presidents have declared a nuclear-armed North Korea to be "intolerable" and "unacceptable." They have repeatedly warned Pyongyang that it cannot export nuclear weapons or technology without facing the "gravest consequences." In 2006, for example, President George W. Bush stated that "the transfer of nuclear weapons or material by North Korea to state or nonstate entities would be considered a grave threat to the United States, and North Korea would be held fully accountable for the consequences." North Korea then proceeded to sell Syria a plutonium-producing reactor that, had Israel not destroyed it, would by now have produced enough plutonium for Syria's first nuclear bomb. Washington's response was to ignore the incident and resume talks three weeks later.

One lesson of the Cuban missile crisis is that if you are not prepared to risk war, even nuclear war, an adroit adversary can get you to back down in successive confrontations. If you do have redlines that would lead to war if crossed, then you have to communicate them credibly to your adversary and back them up or risk having your threats dismissed. North Korea's sale of a nuclear bomb to terrorists who then used it against an American target would trigger a devastating American retaliation. But after so many previous redlines have been crossed with impunity, can one be confident that such a message has been received clearly and convincingly? Could North Korea's new leader, Kim Jong Un, and his advisers imagine that they could get away with it?

THE RULES

A similar dynamic may have emerged in the U.S. economic relationship with China. The Republican presidential candidate Mitt Romney has announced that "on day one of my presidency I will designate [China] a currency manipulator and take appropriate counteraction." The response from the political and economic establishment has been a nearly unanimous rejection of such statements as reckless rhetoric that risks a catastrophic trade war. But if there are no circumstances in which Washington is willing to risk a trade confrontation with China, why would China's leaders not simply take a page from North Korea's playbook? Why should they not continue, in Romney's words, "playing the United States like a fiddle and smiling all the way to the bank" by undervaluing their currency, subsidizing domestic producers, protecting their own markets, and stealing intellectual property through cybertheft?

Economics and security are separate realms, but lessons learned in one can be carried over into the other. The defining geopolitical challenge of the next half century will be managing the relationship between the United States as a ruling superpower and China as a rising one. Analyzing the causes of the Peloponnesian War more than two millennia ago, the Greek historian Thucydides argued that "the growth of the power of Athens, and the alarm which this inspired in Sparta, made war inevitable." During the Cuban missile crisis, Kennedy judged that Khrushchev's adventurism violated what Kennedy called the "rules of the precarious status quo" in relations between two nuclear superpowers. These rules had evolved during previous crises, and the resolution of the standoff in Cuba helped restore and reinforce them, allowing the Cold War to end with a whimper rather than a bang.

The United States and China will have to develop their own rules of the road in order to escape Thucydides' trap. These will need to accommodate both parties' core interests, threading a path between conflict and appeasement. Overreacting to perceived threats would be a mistake, but so would ignoring or papering over unacceptable misbehavior in the hope that it will not recur. In 1996, after some steps by Taipei that Beijing considered provocative, China launched a series of missiles over Taiwan, prompting the United States to send two aircraft carrier battle groups into harm's way. The eventual result was a clearer understanding of both sides' redlines on the Taiwan issue and a calmer region. The relationship may need additional such clarifying moments in order to manage a precarious transition as China's continued economic rise and new status are reflected in expanded military capabilities and a more robust foreign posture.

DO PROCESS

A final lesson the crisis teaches has to do not with policy but with process. Unless the commander in chief has sufficient time and privacy to understand a situation, examine the evidence, explore various options, and reflect before choosing among them, poor decisions are likely. In 1962, one of the first questions Kennedy asked on being told of the missile discovery was, How long until this leaks? McGeorge Bundy, his national security adviser, thought it would be a week at most. Acting on that advice, the president took six days in secret to deliberate, changing his mind more than once along the way. As he noted afterward, if he had been forced to make a decision in the first 48 hours, he would have chosen the air strike rather than the naval blockade—something that could have led to nuclear war.

In today's Washington, Kennedy's week of secret deliberations would be regarded as a relic of a bygone era. The half-life of a hot secret is measured not even in days but in hours. Obama learned this painfully during his first year in office, when he found the administration's deliberations over its Afghanistan policy playing out in public, removing much of his flexibility to select or even consider unconventional options. This experience led him to demand a new national security decision-making process led by a new national security adviser. One of the fruits of the revised approach was a much more tightly controlled flow of information, made possible by an unprecedented narrowing of the inner decision-making circle. This allowed discussions over how to handle the discovery of Osama bin Laden's whereabouts to play out slowly and sensibly, with the sexiest story in Washington kept entirely secret for five months, until the administration itself revealed it after the raid on bin Laden's Abbottabad compound.

It has been said that history does not repeat itself, but it does sometimes rhyme. Five decades later, the Cuban missile crisis stands not just as a pivotal moment in the history of the Cold War but also as a guide for how to defuse conflicts, manage great-power relationships, and make sound decisions about foreign policy in general.

On Humanitarianism

Is Helping Others Charity, or Duty, or Both?

Michael Walzer

Humanitarianism is probably the most important "ism" in the world today, given the collapse of communism, the discrediting of neoliberalism, and the general distrust of large-scale political ideologies. Its activists often claim to escape or transcend partisan politics. We think of humanitarian aid, for example, first of all as a form of philanthropy—a response to an earthquake in Haiti or a tsunami in Asia, which is obviously a good thing, an effort to relieve human suffering and save lives, an act of international benevolence. But there is a puzzle here, for helping people in desperate need is something that we ought to do; it would be wrong not to do it—in which case it is more like justice than benevolence. Words such as "charity" and "philanthropy" describe a voluntary act, a matter of kindness rather than duty. But international humanitarianism seems more like duty than kindness, or maybe it is a combination: two in one, a gift that we have to give.

Individuals send contributions to charitable organizations when there is a humanitarian crisis, and then these organizations rush trained aid workers into the zone of danger and desperate need. But governments also send help, spending tax money that is coercively collected rather than freely given. Are individual citizens

MICHAEL WALZER is Professor Emeritus of Social Science at the Institute for Advanced Study and co-Editor of *Dissent*.

free not to give? Are governments free not to act? Does it matter whether the money is a gift or a tax?

The dilemma is even clearer in the case of humanitarian intervention. Governments may use force to stop a massacre—as France, the United Kingdom, and the United States are claiming to do in Libya and as someone should have done in Rwanda. We can think of this as a gift to the people being rescued, and what is given is substantial, since it may include the lives of some of the interveners. But is the state that intervenes acting charitably? Isn't stopping a massacre morally necessary? And think of the diplomatic preparations for the intervention, the strategic arguments about how to do it, the necessary calculations of proportionality, the marshaling of military resources, the actual use of force, the problems of reconstruction afterward—none of that feels like a philanthropic enterprise. This is more like political work, governed by the rules of justice and prudence, not kindness. And yet, we call it "humanitarian" because we want to believe that what underlies and motivates the intervention, at the deepest level, is human sympathy, freely flowing fellow feeling. It is two in one again: a spontaneous act and a necessary one.

But what if the combination doesn't work—what if the fellow feeling doesn't flow freely?

OBLIGATORY CHARITY

I have been puzzling over these kinds of questions in the course of helping edit a volume in the series *The Jewish Political Tradition*, one dealing with, among other things, charity and taxation—giving and taking. It should be easy to distinguish the two, shouldn't it? Individuals give, freely and spontaneously; the state takes, with threats and penalties. Yet it turns out that the distinction is not so easy to make. The difficulty is signaled by the Hebrew word *tzedakah*, which is commonly translated as "charity" but which comes from the same root as the word for "justice." This suggests that charity is not only good but also right. The same message is conveyed by the Hebrew word mitzvah, which in the Bible means "commandment" but has come colloquially to mean "a good deed" or "an act of human kindness"—although still something that you have to do.

One can see how these versions of the two-in-one argument might develop among a stateless people. With little or no coercive power, the Jewish communities in the Diaspora had to rely heavily on the charitable contributions of their members. The contributions were indeed necessary, for without them there would be no way, for example, to ransom Jewish captives (a major concern of the Diaspora communities throughout the Middle Ages), help the poor and the sick, provide for orphans, or fund synagogues and schools.

And so the medieval philosopher Maimonides argued, following Talmudic precedents, that insofar as Jewish communities in the Diaspora had coercive power, they could legitimately force their members to give *tzedakah*. The *kahal*, the autonomous or semiautonomous Diaspora community, could compel people to give what they were supposed to give freely, and it still counted as a charitable gift. It was distinct (although often hard to distinguish) from the taxes imposed, usually by the gentile overlord, which were levied on individuals by the Jewish rulers of the *kahal*, the *tovei ha-ir* (the good men of the city).

In the Jewish tradition, this view of *tzedakah* as an expression of justice was sometimes described in theological language. The idea is that God has heard and responded to the cries of the poor and, in principle at least, has given them what they need. You may possess some part of what they need, but you possess it only as an agent of God, and if you do not pass it on to the poor, if you do not contribute, say, to the communal charity fund, you are robbing the poor of what in fact already belongs to them. The negative act of not contributing is a positive theft. And since theft is unjust, you are acting not only uncharitably but also unjustly by not giving—which is why coerced *tzedakah* is legitimate. I called this a theological argument, but it is possible even for nonbelievers to accept that, in some sense, it is true and right. Or nonbelievers can translate the argument into secular language: some part of everyone's wealth belongs to the political community, which makes economic activity and peaceful accumulation possible—and it can and should be used to promote the well-being of all the members of the community.

Fundraising in the contemporary Diaspora still partakes of this two-in-one character. I celebrated my bar mitzvah in 1948 in Johnstown, Pennsylvania. That year, my parents brought me with them, as a new member of the community, to the annual banquet of the United Jewish Appeal (UJA), the main fundraising event on the Johnstown Jewish calendar. The year 1948 was a critical one, and every Jew in town was there; no one really had a choice about whether or not to come.There was a speaker from New York who talked with great emotion about the founding of Israel, the war that was then going on, and the desperate needs of the refugees waiting in Europe. Pledge cards were distributed, filled out at the table, and then put in an envelope and passed to the head of the table. There sat the owner of one of the biggest stores in town—let's call him Sam Shapiro. Sam knew everybody else's business: who was doing well and who was not, who was paying college tuition for their children, who had a sick mother, who had recently made a loan to a bankrupt brother, who had money to spare. He opened each envelope, looked at the pledge, and if he thought that it was not enough, he tore the card in half and passed it back down the table. That is how the Jews of Johnstown raised money, without a Jewish state, without—or supposedly without—coercive power. Was that charity, or was it the functional equivalent of taxation? Was it giving, or was it taking? *Tzedakah* signals something of both.

What moral or philosophical principle was Sam enforcing? He probably could not have answered that question, but the answer seems obvious: "from each according to his abilities, to each according to his needs." That line is from Karl Marx's *Critique of the Gotha Program*. Sam was not a Marxist, not by a long shot, but he adjusted the demands he made on each of us to his knowledge of our ability to pay. And we all believed that the UJA would distribute the money to those most in need. "From each, to each" is another example of two in one, for it describes equally well charitable giving and justified taking. This is the principle that Marx believed would apply after the withering away of the state—that is, in a condition of statelessness.

The idea of obligatory charitable giving is not peculiar to the Jews; there are many non-Jewish charities whose staffs would happily collect money the way the Johnstown UJA did, if they could, and would believe themselves to be acting justly. The two-in-one argument comes in Christian and Muslim versions; tithing, for example, is also understood as an act of justice and charity together. But the centuries of statelessness give the Jewish version a special force. Recall the powerful line in the book of Isaiah denouncing those who "grind the faces of the poor." I think of UJA fundraising as grinding the faces of the rich, and although that may or may not be nice, it certainly seems right.

But what should be done with the money collected? What does it mean to address the needs of the poor? This, too, is a question not only of charity but also of justice. Maimonides has a famous discussion of the eight levels of *tzedakah*, but only two need concern us here. The highest form of charitable giving, he wrote, is to set up a poor man in business or in work of some sort, to make him independent. This is the height of *tzedakah* because it recognizes and respects the dignity of the person who is being helped—which is also, obviously, a requirement of justice. When charity perpetuates dependency and subordination, it is unjust. Maimonides also insists that *tzedakah* in its highest form should be anonymous, for if the poor do not know the names of their benefactors, they cannot defer to them. The encounter of helplessness, on one side, and condescending benevolence, on the other, is humiliating for the needy, and so it should be avoided. Here, charitable giving among a stateless people takes on the most important feature of a decent welfare state, where the people receiving benefits are not obligated to any particular benefactor. They are helped as citizens by their fellow citizens, acting collectively.

Tzedakah in actual Jewish communities has often not taken the forms that Maimonides recommended. In many cases, it has been the product of noblesse oblige (which is not the same thing as moral obligation), and there have certainly been many poor people humiliated by gifts for which they had to beg. But the ideal, the collective sense of what *tzedakah* should be, was shaped by the belief that charity had to be governed by the demands of justice. And this two-in-one conception arises from the experience of statelessness.

IDEAL GIVING

Jewish statelessness can help us understand what charity more generally is or should be. It can also provide us with the crucial categories for thinking about humanitarianism in international society. When you do not have a state, charity and justice come two in one. Individuals decide which good deeds, out of many possible ones, they will undertake, which needs they will recognize and how much of their time, energy, and money they will give. But decisions of this sort cannot be made appropriately without understanding what justice requires.

There will be disagreement about what justice requires, of course, and in the absence of a state, there will not be any established procedures for resolving the disagreement—hence, no democratic debates and no democratically chosen policies. And in that situation, the richest and most powerful members of the community will have inordinate influence. Any community that relies heavily on the charitable contributions of its members will be oligarchic in character. It will be ruled by people such as Sam Shapiro, who will sometimes be righteous and kind, as Sam was, and sometimes not.

This is the most important leftist criticism of charity—that it concedes the power of the powerful and forces the poor into the position of beggars. Jewish beggars were known to be unusually demanding, insisting on their entitlements, as if they were expounding the deep meaning of the word *tzedakah*. But they were beggars still. Even when there is a state, but not a fully just state, one that fails to provide generously for education and welfare, the rich and powerful will play a dominant role—as they do, these days, in the United States. Think of the significant role played by the Bill and Melinda Gates Foundation, for example, in shaping the current debate about educational policy, and perhaps determining its outcome, in the United States' inadequately funded public school system.

But if there were a strong and effective welfare state relying on a just system of taxation and taking care of basic needs, then charitable giving would achieve a kind of independence. Now, the giver would be free to follow the impulse of his or her heart, helping other people or improving the common life in any number of ways: volunteering to work in a daycare center, hospital, or nursing home; visiting the sick; supporting charitable projects of a church or synagogue or mosque; giving money to organizations defending civil liberties or human rights; teaching in a local prison or school; contributing to cultural societies, museums, symphonies, and theatrical groups; helping underfunded political magazines.

These choices will have an impact on the quality of life in the larger society, and the accumulation of benevolent acts will shape its overall goodness. But since in our hypothetical good state, the most important decisions about social policy will be made democratically, no individual's choices will have a determining effect. There will be limits on the influence of the rich and powerful. Only in this context would charity mean what we have always taken it to mean: freely chosen acts of kindness, acts that reflect a generosity of spirit, free from the imperatives of justice, free from the urgency of other people's desperate need.

THE POLITICS OF HUMANITARIANISM

In international society, however, there is no global state. Here, the condition of the Jews for 2,000 years is everyone's condition, although it is felt most acutely by those for whom statelessness is doubled, at both the global and the national level—people without a state, or living in failed states, or in states torn by civil wars.

There is no higher authority to which such people can appeal for help. The United Nations sometimes claims to be such an authority, but its repeated failure to rescue those in need of rescuing gives the lie to that claim. The UN Security Council rarely acts effectively in crises, not only because of the veto power of its leading members but also because its members do not have a strong sense of responsibility for global security, for the survival of minority peoples, for public health and environmental safety, or for general well-being. They pursue their own national interests while the world burns.

This is the context in which we have to think about humanitarianism, which cannot in the circumstances of statelessness be a freely chosen gift, which has to respond to urgency and need. It is like *tzedakah*: if it does not connect with justice, it will not be what it should be. Religious men and women can reasonably think that God has already determined what we owe to the global poor, and the sick, and the hungry, and that our task is just to figure it out. And secular men and women can acknowledge that whether or not God exists, this is not a bad way of thinking about these things.

But even when driven by religious motives, humanitarianism is a political project. And because it is, it carries risks with it that are not usually associated with charitable work. Indeed, recent literature on humanitarian aid suggests that the work can go very badly when its organizers are not politically informed, committed to justice, and ready to make prudential calculations. You can, for example, deliver aid in ways that bring in new predators to feed on the provisions and resources intended for the poor, or you can insist on the military or police forces necessary to keep the predators out. You can act through governments that are often corrupt, or you can send your own people into the zones of need and danger and work directly with local individuals and groups. These are choices that primarily involve calculations of effectiveness.

But there are also choices of a different kind. You can help desperately needy people in ways that disempower them and turn them into permanent clients, or you can help them in ways that promote their independence and enable them to help themselves. You can attempt to maintain your political neutrality, or you can take sides in civil wars and ethnic or party conflicts. You can act nonviolently, or you can decide to use or support the use of force. You can aim at relief, or you can aim at repair, sustaining the status quo or trying to transform it. No doubt, different cases require different choices, but in all the cases, these are going to be political choices, and they are likely to be made badly if they are governed chiefly by philanthropic considerations. There is not much room here for post-partisanship. Instead, it is necessary to think about the two-in-one character of humanitarian aid and to ask what justice requires. Similarly, when we judge the value of particular humanitarian projects, we cannot consider only the goodness, the warm-heartedness, the self-sacrifice of the aid workers; we must also ask whether they are acting justly and respectfully toward the people they are trying to help.

Who should make the critical decisions? Who are the agents of international humanitarianism, of charity and justice together? Just as rich and powerful individuals have disproportionate influence in determining the character and direction of domestic philanthropy, we have to worry that the richest and most powerful states and organizations will have a disproportionate influence in determining how aid is delivered and to whom. The big aid organizations are not accountable to the people they claim to help. Won't they often act in their own institutional interests? Don't states always defend their national interests even when they are engaged in humanitarian work?

ASSIGNING RESPONSIBILITY

This seems especially worrisome in the case of humanitarian intervention, which involves the use of force in someone else's country. And indeed, there is a lot of suspicion, especially on the left (but not only there), of any use of force for humanitarian purposes. There are people who claim that all military interventions will inevitably be the work of rich and powerful states acting imperially and will all end in domination. This claim is right—sometimes, which means that it is not inevitably right. Suspicion in these cases invites suspicion in turn, for the original suspicion sometimes follows from a refusal to recognize the extent of the crisis that calls for intervention.

Opposition to all interventions is a mistake, although opposition to some is sure to be morally necessary. Libya may provide a useful example, since the decision to intervene, at the moment it was made, probably did not meet the proportionality test, which is a requirement of justice. And at this moment, as I am writing, the intervention seems to have prolonged, rather than stopped, the killing, which is neither charitable nor just. I doubt that the United States and NATO intend to dominate Libya (for the sake of its oil, say, which was readily available before the intervention). Their motives were and are humanitarian, but not sufficiently shaped by considerations of prudence and justice.

Still, military interventions will sometimes deserve our support, without regard to who the interveners are, so long as they meet the two-in-one criteria. Although we do not want powerful states to dominate international society, we do want access to their resources, precisely to their wealth and power—in the same way that we want access to the resources of wealthy individuals in domestic society, which is why it is right to grind the face of the rich. Charity and justice together require that rich and powerful states contribute disproportionately to the common good or, better, that they contribute in proportion to their disproportionate wealth—"from each, to each." It is more often the case that powerful states don't do enough, or don't do anything at all, in response to desperate need than that they respond in imperialist ways. Humanitarian crises are more often ignored than seized on as an excuse for domination. There cannot be many countries eager to dominate Haiti or Rwanda. So we need to look for ways of pressing rich and powerful states to do what they ought to do.

In fact, there are actually many states in international society that are capable of acting as humanitarian agents. In contrast to ordinary individuals in domestic society, ordinary states, even those far from being great powers, can act effectively in crises because of their ability to collect taxes and recruit aid workers and soldiers. So it is possible to imagine a division of humanitarian labor. Consider the role of the Vietnamese in shutting down the killing fields of the Khmer Rouge in Cambodia, or the Indian role in ending state terrorism in East Pakistan (now Bangladesh), or the role of the Tanzanians in overthrowing the murderous regime of Idi Amin in Uganda. Military intervention in these countries did not require the wealth and power of the United States; it was entirely within the reach of states with much smaller budgets and armies. The case is the same with regard to nonmilitary humanitarian aid, for which many states and many organizations have had a hand in shaping the international efforts—and for which disproportionate influence probably comes more from dedication than from wealth, as the achievements of the Scandinavian states and their aid workers around the world suggest.

Again, this dedication is not merely philanthropic. It arises also from a commitment to justice; like *tzedakah*, it is two in one. And a commitment to justice is not voluntary; it is a commitment that we are all bound to make, as individuals and as citizens, and that all states are bound to make. We are not in a position where we can let generosity and warm-heartedness determine what states do in international society. In the absence of a global welfare state, there are many things that individual states have to do. But here is the agency question again: Which states have to do what?

RELIEF AND REPAIR

International humanitarianism is an imperfect duty. In any crisis situation, different states are capable of acting, but no single state is the designated actor. There is no established procedure that will tell us the proper name of the agent. Aid organizations often respond to a crisis in very large numbers, but without anyone assigned to take charge. The work should be coordinated, for the sake of its effectiveness—and justice requires effectiveness—but there is no named coordinator. We might look for UN designations of responsibility, both when military intervention is called for and when massive aid is called for. But we are likely to look in vain for timely or consistent assignments. In these circumstances, decisions about intervention and aid will often have to be made unilaterally—as by Vietnam, India, and Tanzania in the cases mentioned above. The governing principle is, Whoever can, should.

That is not a principle that can be legally enforced, but there is a political process of enforcement—not very effective, to be sure, but worth considering. It works through public criticism, shaming, moral appeal, and sometimes popular mobilization. The NATO intervention in Kosovo probably had a lot to do with shame over not preventing the Srebrenica massacre; U.S. President Bill Clinton's apology to the people of Rwanda for the United States' failure to prevent the 1994 massacre there was a response of sorts to fierce criticism of the U.S. posture at the UN that year. The unsuccessful campaign for intervention in Darfur involved tens of thousands of activists and sympathizers in a number of countries. This, too, is political work, and what drives it is not only humanitarian benevolence but also a strong sense of what justice requires.

The same combination, two in one, should determine the character and purpose of aid and intervention. It is, of course, immediately necessary to feed the hungry, to stop the killing. Relief comes before repair, but repair, despite the risks it brings with it, should always be the long-term goal—so that crises do not become recurrent and routine. As with *tzedakah* according to Maimonides, aid workers and soldiers should do what they can, the best that they can, to promote the independence of individuals and states. In international society, this means building states that can defend the lives of their citizens and helping them help themselves. What must be avoided is enduring economic or political dependency—the creation of pauper populations or of satellite states and puppet governments. Although we are often told that the state system must be transcended, sovereignty is in fact humanitarianism's morally necessary end: a decent state, capable of providing security, welfare, economic management, and education for all its citizens. Then, the aid workers and the intervening armies can go home. If they have created the conditions for self-determination, we know that they have acted both charitably and justly.

So state building can be a form of humanitarian work, even though we don't know anywhere near enough about how to do it. Regime change, however, is something different. When the Red Army tried to bring communism to Poland in 1919 and when the U.S. Army tried to bring democracy to Iraq in 2003 (and to Libya in 2011?), these were ideological, not humanitarian, projects. They aimed at repair but not at relief, whereas humanitarianism aims at repair only after, and in order to sustain, relief. It is the critical need for relief that generates the two-in-one response that we call humanitarian.

Relief and repair can take a long time, and there will be hard choices to make along the way, without any international procedure for making them. There is also no legal way to conscript people or states to do the necessary work or to regulate the work they do. That is, again, what global statelessness means. And so we must search for more informal ways of pressing people into humanitarian service and evaluating and criticizing what they do (and don't do). Since there are few effective laws in international society, we need principles of charity and justice that will shape our own contributions and also our judgments of what other people contribute.

Humanitarianism has to be an ongoing argument: What ought to be done right now? The answer to that question will change depending on the existing needs, the political circumstances, the resources that benevolence can provide, and the requirements of justice. But once we have figured out an answer, we can think of humanitarianism as the two-in-one enterprise that I have been describing. As individual men and women, as members of or contributors to nongovernmental organizations, as citizens of powerful states, it invites us to choose to do what we are absolutely bound to do.

God and Caesar in America

Why Mixing Religion and Politics Is Bad for Both

David E. Campbell and Robert D. Putnam

From the day the Pilgrims stepped off the Mayflower, religion has played a prominent role in American public life. The faithful have been vital participants in nearly every major social movement in U.S. history, progressive as well as conservative. Still, the close intertwining of religion and politics in the last 40 years is unusual, especially in the degree of the politicization of religion itself. Indeed, religion's influence on U.S. politics has hit a high-water mark, especially on the right. Yet at the same time, its role in Americans' personal lives is ebbing. As religion and politics have become entangled, many Americans, especially younger ones, have pulled away from religion. And that correlation turns out to be causal, not coincidental.

DAVID E. CAMPBELL is John Cardinal O'Hara, C.S.C. Associate Professor of Political Science and Director of the Rooney Center for the Study of American Democracy at the University of Notre Dame.

ROBERT D. PUTNAM is Peter and Isabel Malkin Professor of Public Policy at Harvard University. This essay is adapted from the paperback edition of their book, *American Grace* (Simon & Schuster, 2012).

It is no surprise that religion and politics should be connected to some degree in a highly religious and democratic nation. In the nineteenth century, U.S. political parties were divided along sectarian lines: pietistic versus liturgical, low church versus high church, Protestant versus Catholic. But whereas the past saw partisans of different religions (often with an ethnic tinge) face off in the political arena, today partisan divisions are not defined by denomination; rather, they pit religiously devout conservatives against secular progressives. Moreover, to a degree not seen since at least the 1850s (and perhaps not even then), religious mobilization is now tied directly to party politics.

In fact, over the last 20 years, church attendance has become the main dividing line between Republican and Democratic voters. (African Americans are a sharp, but singular, exception; although most Democratic voters are now secular, African Americans, the most loyal Democrats, are also the most religious group in the United States.) The so-called God gap, between churchgoing Republicans and secular white Democrats, rose sharply throughout the 1990s and early years of this century. Before the 2008 presidential election, one team of consultants even specialized in teaching Democratic candidates how to "do God," so they could eat into the Republicans' support among religious Americans. Yet in 2008, the God gap remained as wide as ever: according to data we collected, among whites, 67 percent of weekly churchgoers voted for Senator John McCain, as compared with 26 percent of those who never attended church.

The connection between religiosity and political conservatism has become so deeply embedded in contemporary U.S. culture that it is startling to recall just how new the alignment is. In the 1960s, churchgoers were actually more likely than nonchurchgoers to be Democrats. Into the 1980s, there were still plenty of progressives in the pews on Sunday morning and plenty of conservatives who stayed home. The rather sudden shift since then has, and will have, both short-term and long-term implications for both politics and religion. For now, Republicans must seek to appease their fervently religious base without alienating a general electorate that increasingly finds the mixture of religion and politics distasteful. In the long run, the trend could undermine the historic role of religion in the United States, as younger generations reject organized religion itself. The country has arrived at today's close nexus between religion and partisanship only recently, and understanding how it got there—and how the role of religion in the United States has changed in recent decades—will help explain where it might be headed.

IN THE BEGINNING

To get a better sense of how novel the present political-religious landscape is, we must go back to the 1950s. That decade was highly religious; indeed, some historians argue that it was the most religious in all of American history. Of course, there are many ways to gauge national trends in religiosity, but for decades, one Gallup poll question, "Is religion's influence on American life increasing or decreasing?" has proved a finely tuned seismometer of religious tremors. In 1957, 69 percent of those Americans surveyed told Gallup that they thought the influence of religion in American life was on the rise. Only 14 percent said it was declining. Every objective measure indicates that they were right: more Americans than ever were attending religious services, more churches were being built to accommodate them, and more books of Scripture were being sold and read. But in President Dwight Eisenhower's America, religion had no partisan overtones. Ike was as popular among those who never darkened the door of a church (or synagogue, and so on) as among churchgoers.

Then came the 1960s, and a dramatic turn in attitudes toward authority and especially toward conventional sexual morality, an issue tightly connected to religious belief. In just four years, between 1969 and 1973, the percentage of Americans who approved of premarital sex doubled, from one-fourth to one-half. That increase was stunning and almost entirely concentrated among the baby boomers, who were then coming of age. By 1970, fully 75 percent of

Americans surveyed concluded that religion's influence in American life was waning. Collapsing church attendance confirmed their view. Yet even then, religiosity did not skew more to the right than the left; neither during the religious boom of the 1950s nor in the religious bust of the 1960s was religion linked to partisan politics.

Nor did the 1960s put the United States on an inexorable path toward secularism. Far from it: instead, among more conservative Americans, the moral earthquake triggered a return to religion, or at least a particular type of religion. Beginning in the mid-1970s, in an aftershock to the 1960s, conservative forms of religion, especially evangelical Protestantism, expanded. At the same time as liberal Protestantism and churchgoing Catholicism were virtually collapsing, many Americans who sought a reaffirmation of traditional norms, especially when it came to sex and "family values," found what they were looking for in evangelical Protestantism. The new evangelicals also broke free of the self-imposed cultural exile of their fundamentalist forebears. They did not shun a sinful world but instead sought to change it, including its politics.

An early harbinger of evangelicalism's new political role was the 1976 presidential campaign of the Democrat Jimmy Carter, who spoke openly of himself as a "born-again Christian," a label once unthinkable in mainstream U.S. politics. At the other end of the political spectrum, meanwhile, moral conservatives banded together to fight the Equal Rights Amendment, gay rights, and abortion. Evangelicalism began morphing from a purely religious movement into a political one that allied devout Americans from many denominations, including Catholics and Mormons. Once more, Gallup's seismometer noted the increasing prominence of religion. In 1976, it registered that 44 percent of respondents thought religion was gaining influence, and 45 percent thought it was losing influence.

Then, in his 1980 presidential campaign, the Republican Ronald Reagan actively courted the religious vote with considerable success. Unlike Eisenhower in the 1950s or even Presidents Richard Nixon and Gerald Ford in the 1970s, Reagan and the Republican presidential candidates that followed him began to pick up the support of formerly Democratic evangelicals in the South and observant Catholics in the North.

The first aftershock to the 1960s thus had two components: one religious (the rise of evangelicals) and the other political (the rise of the religious right). The political movement continues, but the religious dimension ended in the early 1990s. As a fraction of the total population (and, even more dramatically, as a fraction of Americans under 30), the number of evangelicals has been declining for nearly 20 years and is back to where it was at the beginning of the 1970s.

Although many of the political organizations associated with the religious right, such as the Moral Majority and the Christian Coalition, have disappeared or faded into near irrelevance, their legacy remains strong: a Republican activist base that advocates both moral traditionalism and a greater role for religion in the public square.

The rise of the religious right echoes in some respects a common theme in U.S. history. Most major social movements, both progressive and conservative, have included important religious themes: "the right to life" and "family values" today, abolitionism and prohibition yesterday. But today's unusually intimate ties between organized religion and one particular political party have had unintended consequences for both politics and religion.

THE GOD-GIVEN RIGHT

With the rise of the religious right came the much-discussed God gap between Republicans and Democrats. Each year, fewer and fewer Americans identify as secular Republicans or religious Democrats. What happened to those who once did? Did they adjust their politics to fit their religion, or vice versa? Surprisingly, politics has mostly determined religious practice. Formerly religious Democrats (except among African Americans) have drifted away from church, and formerly unobservant Republicans have found religion.

Take the Tea Party. Even this ostensibly secular movement has strong religious undertones. A large, nationally representative survey that we first conducted in 2006 (before the Tea Party was formed) and repeated with the same respondents in 2011 casts doubt on the conventional wisdom about the movement's origin. In its early days, the Tea Party was often described as comprising nonpartisan political neophytes who, hurt by the Great Recession, had been spurred into action out of concern over runaway government spending. This is a triple myth. In reality, those Americans who support the Tea Party were (and remain) overwhelmingly partisan Republicans. They were politically active even in the pre-Tea Party days, and they were no more likely than anyone else to have suffered hardship during the recent economic downturn.

Indeed, it turns out that the strongest predictor of a Republican becoming a Tea Party supporter is whether he or she evinced a desire in our 2006 survey to see religion play a prominent role in politics. And that desire does not simply reflect members' high religiosity. Tea Partiers are, on average, more religiously observant than the typical American, but not more so than other Republicans. Rather, they are distinctively comfortable blending religion and politics. Tea Partiers are more likely than other Republicans to say that U.S. laws and policies would be better if the country had more "deeply religious" elected officials, that it is appropriate for religious leaders to engage in political persuasion, and that religion should be brought into public debates over political issues. The Tea Party's generals might say that their overriding concern is smaller government, but the rank and file is after a godlier government.

Tea Partiers' views in this respect are increasingly out of step with those of most Americans. According to Gallup polls, as early as 1984, just as the alliance between religious and political conservatives was crystallizing, most Americans opposed the idea of religious groups campaigning against specific candidates. Moreover, according to the widely respected national General Social Survey, as the public visibility of the religious right increased between 1991 and 2008, growing numbers of Americans expressed the conviction that religious leaders should not try to influence people's votes or government decisions. In 1991, 22 percent of those surveyed said they "strongly agree" that religious leaders should not try to influence government decisions; by 2008, that figure had nearly doubled, to 38 percent. In our 2011 survey, 80 percent of respondents said that it is not proper for religious leaders to tell people how to vote, and 70 percent said that religion should be "kept out of public debates over social and political issues."

It should thus come as no surprise that many Americans have negative views of the Tea Party. In the same 2011 poll, the Tea Party ranked at the bottom of a list of two dozen U.S. religious, political, and racial groups in terms of favorability. (It was even less liked than Muslims and atheists, two groups that regularly meet with public opprobrium.) One of the few groups approaching the unpopularity of the Tea Party was the religious right. Both movements (which overlap heavily) might have won the staunch support of a minority of American voters, but they have also won the staunch opposition of a much larger group.

This shift has created a dilemma for Republican candidates seeking the Tea Partiers' support. Not only must Republicans toe the conservative line on fiscal issues, immigration, and national security, but Tea Party sympathizers (who compose barely a quarter of the national electorate but more than half of the Republican primary electorate) also expect them to favor a fusion of religion and politics. The problem for the Republican Party is that this fusion is unpopular among the general electorate and is becoming more so. Thus, as culture warriors fire up the Republican base, they leave independent voters cold. In contrast, more centrist candidates are attractive to the moderate middle but win only tepid support among the activists who want more God in government.

LOSING MY RELIGION

The consequences of the melding of religion and party politics extend beyond electoral politics; the commingling has also reshaped the United States' religious landscape. Just as the 1960s spurred a revival of traditional religion, the last few decades have led directly to an unprecedented turning away from organized religion, especially among younger Americans.

Consider the growth in the number of people whom sociologists call "nones," those who report no religious affiliation. Historically, this category made up a constant 5-7 percent of the American population, even during the 1960s, when religious attendance dropped. In the early 1990s, however, just as the God gap widened in politics, the percentage of nones began to shoot up. By the mid-1990s, nones made up 12 percent of the population. By 2011, they were 19 percent. In demographic terms, this shift was huge. To put the figures in context, in the two decades between the early 1970s and the early 1990s, the heyday of evangelicalism, the fraction of the population that was evangelical grew by only about five percentage points. The percentage of nones grew twice as much in the last two decades and is still climbing. Moreover, the rise is heavily concentrated among people under 30, the so-called millennial generation. To be sure, the young are always less religiously observant than their elders; people tend to become more religious when they get married, have children, and put down roots in a community (demographers call this the life-cycle effect). Yet 20-somethings in 2012 are much more likely to reject all religious affiliation than their parents and grandparents were when they were young—33 percent today, compared with 12 percent in the 1970s.

The millennials' movement away from organized religion has recently accelerated. Between 2006 and 2011, the fraction of nones in the population as a whole rose modestly, from 17 percent to 19 percent. Among younger Americans, however, the fraction increased approximately five times as much. Similarly, over the same five-year period, the fraction of Americans who reported never attending religious services rose by a negligible two percentage points among Americans over the age of 60 but by three times as much among those 18-29. And younger millennials are even more secular than their slightly older siblings; our 2011 survey showed that a third of Americans in their early 20s were without religion, compared with a quarter of those who were that age when we surveyed them in 2006.

The Gallup religious seismometer has signaled a plunge in religion's influence in American life, too. And in our survey, Americans of all walks of life, religious and secular, white and nonwhite, rich and poor, urban and rural, liberal and conservative, old and young, highly educated and less educated, reported the shift in about equal measure. Since we interviewed the very same people in 2006 and 2011, we can even see large numbers of individuals lowering their own estimates of religion's role in American life.

The best evidence indicates that this dramatic generational shift is primarily in reaction to the religious right. Politically moderate and progressive Americans have a general allergy to the mingling of religion and party politics. And millennials are even more sensitive to it, partly because many of them are liberal (especially on the touchstone issue of gay rights) and partly because they have only known a world in which religion and the right are intertwined. To them, "religion" means "Republican," "intolerant," and "homophobic." Since those traits do not represent their views, they do not see themselves—or wish to be seen by their peers—as religious.

Our data support this theory. By tracking individuals for five years, between 2006 and 2011, we found that Democrats and progressives were much more likely to become nones than were Republicans. The religious defections were concentrated specifically among those Americans who reported the greatest discomfort with religion-infused politics, regardless of their own partisan loyalties. In effect, Americans (especially young Americans) who might otherwise attend religious services are saying, "Well, if religion is just about conservative politics, then I'm outta here."

These data point to a rich irony about the emergence of the religious right. Its founders intended to bolster religion's place in the public square. In a sense, they have succeeded. Yet at the same time, in a classic demonstration of the danger of unintended consequences, the movement has pushed a growing share of the population to opt out of religion altogether.

FOR GOD'S SAKE

American religious groups have historically been distinctive in their adaptability and self-correcting tendencies. Rather than signaling the certain death of religion, our 2011 nationwide survey found hints that, feeling the heat from their too close association with partisan politics, religious leaders are beginning to pull back. Indeed, one of the most significant differences between our 2006 and our 2011 data was the drop-off in political activity within U.S. religious congregations. In 2006, 32 percent of Americans who belonged to a congregation reported hearing sermons with political content "once every month or two" or "several times a month." By 2011, that figure had fallen to 19 percent. The trend held among those of all religious traditions, in all regions of the country, among conservatives and liberals, young and old, and urban and rural. Presumably, clergy across the country have sensed what we see in the data, namely, Americans' growing aversion to blurring the lines between God and Caesar. So they have opted to stick to God.

The decrease in politicking from the pulpit will likely not have an immediate effect on the God gap. The chasm has become a fixture of the U.S. party system and is likely to persist in the short term, barring a sweeping political realignment. However, if clergy continue to retreat from politics, candidates of the religious right will have fewer opportunities to tap into church-based social networks for political mobilization. And if Republicans continue their exclusive alignment with organized religion, they will encounter ever more resistance from moderate voters, especially in the younger generation, who are in their politically formative years now and will be around for a long time.

Future historians may well see the last third of the twentieth century as an anomaly, a period in which religion and public life in the United States became too partisan for the good of either. Republican politicians facing the loss of the religiously moderate middle and pastors seeing a rapid graying of their dwindling flock are both paying a belated but serious price for the religious right's dip into politics. Beyond that, all sides—progressive and conservative, religious and secular—should be concerned that placing a partisan label on religion has hurt the ability of religious leaders to summon moral arguments on behalf of causes that transcend left and right. Martin Luther King, Jr.'s prophetic call for racial justice was persuasive in part because his words and deeds drew on powerful religious symbolism that could not be reduced to base partisanship. Indeed, religion has historically inspired change across the U.S. political spectrum. American public discourse—and the country at large—will be impoverished if religion is reduced to a mere force for partisan mobilization.